Precious BLOOD

Precious BLOOD
THE ATONING WORK OF CHRIST

EDITED BY

RICHARD D. PHILLIPS

CROSSWAY BOOKS

WHEATON, ILLINOIS

Precious Blood: The Atoning Work of Christ
Copyright © 2009 by Alliance of Confessing Evangelicals
Published by Crossway Books
          a publishing ministry of Good News Publishers
          1300 Crescent Street
          Wheaton, Illinois 60187

Cover design: Amy Bristow
Interior design and typesetting: Lakeside Design Plus
First printing 2009

Unless otherwise indicated, Scripture quotations are from the ESV® Bible (*The Holy Bible, English Standard Version®*), copyright © 2001 by Crossway Bibles, a publishing ministry of Good News Publishers. Used by permission. All rights reserved.

Scripture quotations marked KJV are from the *King James Version* of the Bible.

All emphases in Scripture quotations have been added by the author.

Trade paperback ISBN: 978-1-4335-0921-6
PDF ISBN: 978-1-4335-0922-3
Mobipocket ISBN: 978-1-4335-0923-0

Library of Congress Cataloging-in-Publication Data
Philadelphia Conference on Reformed Theology (2008)
    Precious blood : the atoning work of Christ / Richard D. Phillips, editor.
        p. cm.
    Includes bibliographical references and index.
    ISBN 978-1-4335-0921-6 (tpb)
    1. Atonement—Congresses. I. Phillips, Richard D. (Richard Davis),
1960– II. Title.

BT265.3.P45 2008
232'.3—dc22
                                         2008048197

VP   19 18 17 16 15 14 13 12 11 10 09
14 13 12 11 10 9 8 7 6 5 4 3 2 1

To
Elmer Snethen
Faithful Brother, Leader, and Servant in Christ
(Prov. 17:17)

and

Him
Who loves us and has freed us from our sins by his blood
(Rev. 1:5)

CONTENTS

PREFACE

Wash thee in Christ's blood, which hath this might
That being red, it dyes red soules to white.

—John Donne, *La Corona*

At the very heart of our Christian faith is a precious red substance: the blood of our Lord Jesus Christ. The sin-atoning death of Christ is remarkable for being at once most offensive to the world, most treasured by the church, most astonishing to the mind, and most stirring to the soul. Simply put, the one thing we would least expect to hear about God is that he sent his own Son to die for our sins. Thus it is Christ's precious blood that puts the amazing into grace, puts the wonderful into the gospel, and puts the marvelous into God's plan of salvation. There can be no greater truth to be faced than the gospel message of the cross, no greater mystery to be considered, and no greater comfort to be received. The cross is a theme that Christians will meditate on forever without exhausting its wonder, and of the cross God's redeemed will sing with glorious praise to unending ages.

With this in mind, this volume seeks to set forth for our generation the doctrine of Christ's atonement. There are any number of good reasons to study the atonement. First, the cross is the divine work on which the entire structure of our salvation rests and the truth on which our doctrine of salvation must be built. Along with the inerrancy of Scripture, the doctrine of Christ's penal substitutionary atonement has been for generations the linchpin of evangelical Christianity. But recent years have seen a pastoral neglect of the cross and an increasingly intense doctrinal assault from academia. This gives us a second important reason to return to the atonement: if Christians are to have any faith to defend at all, we will have to defend our gospel here.

Third, there is a perennial need to proclaim and explain the doctrinal categories associated with the cross in the Bible. What are atonement, substitution, redemption, propitiation, expiation, and reconciliation? Every generation must teach these truths from God's Word and do so frequently.

It was to this end that the contributors to this volume gathered in the spring of 2008 for the annual Philadelphia Conference on Reformed Theology, seeking to refresh the souls and minds of veteran believers and to instruct and inspire those coming to grips with the cross for the first time. The plenary sessions of the conference focused on the biblical doctrine of the blood of Christ, and the seminars set forth theological reflection on the atonement over the course of church history, from the early church to today. These two foci provide the two main sections of this book, Part 1 setting forth the biblical revelation concerning Christ's blood and Part 2 considering the atonement in Christian thought.

Having the honor of editing this volume of outstanding contributions, I pray for God to bless these studies for the upbuilding of the readers' faith in Christ and for the extension of God's glory in the world. The matters discussed in this book are of the most vital importance, and I believe them to be among the truths most blessed and cherished by God himself.

I wish to convey my thanks to the contributors, to Allan Fisher and his wonderful colleagues at Crossway Books, and to my dear friends Bob Brady and the staff of the Alliance of Confessing Evangelicals. I also am grateful to the session and congregation of Second Presbyterian Church, Greenville, South Carolina, for their loving support of my ministry of teaching and writing, and most importantly to my dearly beloved wife and our children, whose devotion to my calling to Christ involves numerous and regular sacrifices on their part.

This volume is dedicated with loving appreciation to Elmer Snethen, longtime chairman of the board of the Alliance of Confessing Evangelicals, for his devoted service, his effective leadership, and most importantly for his tender love that always exudes the aroma of the cross of Christ.

—Richard D. Phillips
Greenville, South Carolina
October 2008

PART I

THE *Atonement*
IN BIBLICAL REVELATION

NECESSARY BLOOD

Joel R. Beeke

The blood shall be to you for a token upon the houses where ye are: and when I see the blood, I will pass over you, and the plague shall not be upon you to destroy you, when I smite the land of Egypt.

—Exodus 12:13[1]

Israel's dramatic deliverance from Egypt was so miraculous that God's people would often look back on this extraordinary event with astonishment. The crisis recorded in Exodus 12 resulted in a national deliverance for Israel but a national disaster for Egypt. For both nations, it was an unforgettable night. Great deliverance came for Israel; the judgments of God that came so heavily on Egypt, killing all firstborn sons, passed over the homes of the children of God. Israel called that night Passover because God's angel of death passed over the homes of God's people. God gave detailed instructions about how to celebrate that occasion, which they called the Feast of the Passover.

The Passover Feast

As we begin our studies of the biblical presentation of Christ's atoning blood, perhaps the best place to start is with the Old Testament, for the cross of Christ did not appear out of thin air. Instead, the blood of Christ was shed amidst the richest biblical context. Indeed,

evangelical Christians see the cross as fulfilling the very heart of the
Hebrew Scripture's expectation. It is from the Old Testament that
we gain the clearest perspective of the necessity of Christ's blood.
All through the Old Testament, especially in its greatest redemptive
event, the exodus, God presses upon us our absolute need for atoning
blood for the forgiveness of our sins.

Passover meant a great deal to Old and New Testament saints,
including our Lord Jesus Christ, who faithfully observed this feast
each year. Several of Christ's significant addresses to his disciples
were given at the Feast of the Passover.

The original Passover was both a day of judgment and a day of
salvation. Exodus 12 shows how God sheltered his people and kept
them secure from judgment. What, precisely, made God's people so
secure? What preserved them from the solemn judgment that extended
over the entire land of Egypt?

God made a distinction between Egypt and Israel for a specific
reason. The distinction was not one of race or nation, class or privilege. It was a distinction of blood. God told them to take a lamb
and sprinkle its blood on "the two side posts and on the upper door
post of the houses, wherein they shall eat it" (v. 7). Verse 13 goes on
to say, "And the blood shall be to you for a token upon the houses
where ye are: and when I see the blood, I will pass over you, and the
plague shall not be upon you to destroy you, when I smite the land
of Egypt." The people of God were sheltered under the blood of the
lamb. Blood was the distinctive mark that saved them.

This blood points to Christ as God's Lamb. We need to remind
ourselves that much of the Old Testament, Exodus in particular, is God's
great picture book in which he illustrates in shadow and type what he
is going to do at the most crucial hour of all history, when the Messiah
comes. The crux of Christ's ministry is when he, as the Paschal Lamb,
fulfills everything that God so clearly points to in the Old Testament.

At the original Passover, God did far more than deliver Israel
from Egypt. He taught them the way of salvation. He used this

physical, external, and national deliverance to teach each Israelite about spiritual and eternal deliverance. No one was saved from sin or from hell by observing the Passover; the blood of bulls, goats, and lambs could never wash away sin, as Hebrews 10:4 tells us. So God took this external, physical ritual of deliverance to teach Israel about spiritual, internal, and eternal deliverance. The Passover is thus a kind of visual aid. In it God illustrates the way of salvation, foreshadowing the great act of redemption that Christ will accomplish. And in it God also pictures the internal response, or the experiential side of salvation.

The New Testament makes it clear that the paschal lamb of Passover is an image that points to Jesus Christ, in whom believers find the whole of their salvation. Thus John the Baptist began his earthly ministry by crying out, "Behold the Lamb of God, which taketh away the sin of the world" (John 1:29). Even more pointedly, Paul writes, "Christ our passover is sacrificed for us: therefore let us keep the feast" (1 Cor. 5:7–8). And when Peter speaks of Christ's redeeming blood, he says that it is as the blood of a lamb without blemish or spot (1 Pet. 1:19).

Christ is our Passover Lamb, the only perfect wrath-appeasing, justice-satisfying Lamb. Nothing was more important for Israel than the lamb God provided, the blood of which sheltered them personally and experientially from death. And nothing is more necessary for us today than the precious blood of the Lamb of God, which shelters us from eternal death.

Exodus 12 tells us four significant things about the Passover lamb, all of which are fulfilled in Christ. The Passover story is told in Exodus 12:3–14, centering on this great gospel promise: "And the blood shall be to you for a token upon the houses where ye are: and when I see the blood, I will pass over you, and the plague shall not be upon you to destroy you, when I smite the land of Egypt" (Ex. 12:13). In the Passover account, we should especially observe four features, each of which amplifies the necessity of Christ's atoning blood for us: (1) the choosing of the lamb; (2) the sprinkled blood of the lamb; (3) eating the supper of the lamb; and (4) following the way of the lamb.

Choosing the Lamb

Exodus 12 tells us the Passover lamb had to be chosen deliberately and carefully. Israel could not use just any lamb for Passover. The lamb had to meet several qualifications. First, the lamb had to meet *the requirements of God*. Thus, it had to be a *spotless lamb*. Verse 5 says, "Your lamb shall be without blemish, a male of the first year: ye shall take it out from the sheep, or from the goats." We are told in Leviticus 22:22–23 what a blemish-free lamb was like. It could not have a crooked nose, a broken hoof, or any scurvy on its skin. Nothing could be superfluous on this lamb, nor could anything be lacking in its parts. Nothing in this lamb could offend God. It had to be perfect.

Likewise, the New Testament takes great pains to tell us that Christ our Passover Lamb is a perfect offering for the sins of his people. He is holy, harmless, and undefiled. He is the Lamb of God without spot and blemish, fully acceptable to God. This perfection is critical, for no sacrifice for sin is possible other than the perfect sacrifice that God ordained in Exodus and fulfilled in Jesus. This is why the Bible stresses Jesus' perfect, obedient life as well as his perfect, sacrificial death. And this is why the New Testament stresses Jesus' sinlessness, his moral perfection, and his unconditional obedience to his Father in every stage of his ministry. This perfect obedience, however costly it was at various points in Jesus' life, was the very essence of his becoming our Savior. The Father required a perfect offering for the satisfaction of our sins, which Christ alone could give as the perfect Lamb of God.

The lesson this teaches us is one that should be rooted deeply in every believer's soul: *no offering other than Jesus is acceptable to God*. We remember how Abraham tried to bring some other offering into God's presence besides Isaac, whose sacrifice God had commanded. Abraham said, "O that Ishmael might live before thee!" (Gen. 17:18). Abraham tried to find another way to please God, but God utterly rejected it. Likewise today, when we try to find a way other than Christ to have our sins washed away, God utterly rejects every one of those ways.

Do you clearly understand the necessity of Christ for your eternal salvation? Have you been weaned away from all righteousness that is not Christ's? Are you resting only on the perfect Lamb of God? Have you experienced that none of your Ishmaels, none of your works, are good enough to pay the price of sin? Are you persuaded that only Christ can unlock the gate of salvation for you?

Second, the lamb had to meet *the needs of the people*. This meant two things. First, the lamb had to be killed as a substitute for the death of the people. According to Exodus 12:3–4, this need was carefully counted and measured:

> Speak ye unto all the congregation of Israel, saying, In the tenth day of this month they shall take to them every man a lamb, according to the house of their fathers, a lamb for an house: and if the household be too little for the lamb, let him and his neighbour next unto his house take it according to the number of the souls; every man according to his eating shall make your count for the lamb.

Israel was a sinful nation. Every Israelite was condemned before God. In themselves, Israelites were no different from the Egyptians. Their only hope was that God would meet their need for salvation by providing a lamb that would die in their place, pointing to the Messiah who was to come.

God decreed that the Passover lamb had to meet the needs of his people perfectly. The people broke the law, but the Messiah Lamb will fulfill it. The people are sinners, but the Messiah Lamb pays for every sin. The people are weak, but the Messiah Lamb is strong. The people are foolish, but the Messiah Lamb is wise. The people are often prayerless, but the Messiah Lamb is an interceding high priest. The people are plagued by sin's debt, but the Lamb of God pays the full price for all their sins. In Christ, God's people find mercy based on justice; in Christ, they find salvation by vicarious sacrifice. They deserve to be destroyed, but Christ willingly takes their place.

Have you experienced that you are worthy of condemnation before God and in need of a righteousness better than your own? Have you realized that, without the blood of Christ, you must confess, "If God should mark iniquity, I could never stand. Hell would be my portion forever"? Can you say with Horatius Bonar:

> I lay my sins on Jesus,
> The spotless Lamb of God,
> He bears them all and frees us
> From the accursed load;
> I lay my wants on Jesus,
> All fullness dwells in Him.[2]

Have you then come to rejoice in salvation, confessing, "Thanks be to God, Jesus Christ is a vicarious sacrifice for me, the perfect Savior I need"?

A second way the lamb's choice meets the people's need is by the way it was tested. The lamb could not be chosen in a moment of panic on the night when judgment was about to fall. It had to be chosen when people had time to observe the lamb's qualifications. Exodus 12:6 says, "And ye shall keep it up until the fourteenth day of the same month." There were two important reasons for this.

First, the lamb had to prove under detailed scrutiny that it was *without blemish*. Each family picked out an unblemished lamb from their flock before the Passover. They separated it from the flock and took it home. For fourteen days the family fed and cared for the lamb. The little children probably came up to the little animal to pet it and feed it. Gradually, the lamb became part of the family. This was to teach the Israelites that the coming Messiah, like this lamb, would be separate from the people and yet, as a perfect animal, come to live among them to be their Savior.

Christ was under observation for thirty-three years. No one could find any blemish in him during those years. He could say to his accusers, "Which of you convinceth me of sin?" (John 8:46). Hebrews 4:15 says that Christ was associated with us and yet separate from us, being tempted in all points as we are, yet without sin. He was the Holy One brought forth from the Virgin Mary (Luke 1:35). Even Pilate, handing Jesus over to death, had to confess, "I find in him no fault at all" (John 18:38). We can thus be confident that God is satisfied with the sacrifice of Jesus Christ.

Moreover, the lamb had to be tested so that the people of God would be *prepared for the feast*. The children of Israel were not to rush out on the night of the judgment to see if they had a lamb fit for the Passover. That provision was to be secured well before the night of judgment.

This raises the question if you are ready for God's coming judgment. Do you have the Lamb of God's provision to present to God? A young man once said to me, when I urged him to seek the Lord, "Sometime I will think seriously about the things of God; but not now. I have too much to do." That young man died shortly thereafter.

You and I must make sure today that we are sheltered under the Messiah's blood—that we have chosen and embraced by gracious faith the tested Lamb that perfectly meets God's requirements and our needs. We must be able to sing from the heart:

> *None other lamb, none other name,*
> *None other hope in heaven or after see,*
> *None other hiding place from guilt or shame,*
> *None beside Thee, none beside Thee.[3]*

Sprinkling the Blood

On the night of Passover, all the men in Israel acted in unison in their respective homes. Each man took his lamb, pulled back the animal's neck, and slit its throat. The blood gushed everywhere. What a solemn, unforgettable time this was for the Israelites!

Then, as Exodus 12:7 says, the men took the blood of the slaughtered lamb and sprinkled it "on the two side posts and on the upper door post of the houses, wherein they shall eat it." Then, as verse 22 tells us, the men and their households stayed at home all night. They remained there, sheltered under the blood.

What a vivid picture this is of God's covenantal salvation provided for Israel! The household context reinforces the covenant pattern of believers and their offspring. And the choice of the door, or way of access, as the place for the blood to be spattered, reminds us of Christ's own saying that he is the door (John 10:1–3).

You can imagine the scene, can't you? The Israelites killed their lambs and sprinkled the doorposts of their houses red. This was not done in secret but was a public profession of faith in the blood the Lord provided for their deliverance. Some Egyptians might have passed by, laughing at the sight and asking, "Why are you painting blood on your houses? How do you think the blood of a lamb will save you? Don't be ridiculous!" That mockery echoes throughout the ages. The bloody, crucified Christ is foolishness to men but the power of God unto salvation.

What an act of faith it took to sprinkle this blood! It seemed so ineffectual. How could the spattering of blood deliver from death? The reason behind it, however, was simple: God had commanded it. Judgment was coming. This is what God commanded for the people to be delivered from judgment.

And so the Israelites stayed under the shelter of blood all that night. When a child would ask, "Daddy, what is God teaching us about this? What does this mean?" the father would respond, "It means that eventually the blood of the Messiah will be shed to take away sin. We must take shelter under that. We are to profess it publicly. However illogical it seems, even to us, we know that we are saved from the wrath of God by the precious blood of the Lamb. That is our only hope."

God specifically required the blood of the lamb. Blood means life offered up, life sacrificed in death. The lamb was appointed for judgment and to satisfy justice. Just as judgment went out over the firstborn of Egypt that night, so judgment fell on every lamb that had been chosen—perfect and without blemish—in every house of God's chosen Israel.

This blood spoke in two directions: upward to God and outward to men. In Exodus 12:13 God says, "And the blood shall be to you for a token upon the houses where ye are: and when *I* see the blood, *I* will pass over you." God's wrath was appeased by the blood of the lamb. The only thing that would hold the angel of death back from entering a home and killing the firstborn was the blood of a spotless lamb.

This is precisely the significance of Jesus' blood in the Bible. The blood of Jesus still speaks to his Father in heaven. It reaches up to the throne of God and touches the heart of God, turning aside his wrath and judgment. The blood of Jesus alone can do that. That is why the Bible says that the blood of Jesus speaks better things than the blood of Abel (Heb. 12:24).

This blood also speaks to sinners. Exodus 12:13 says, "And the blood shall be to *you* for a token upon the houses where ye are: and when I see the blood, I will pass over *you*, and the plague shall not be upon *you* to destroy *you*, when I smite the land of Egypt." Verse 23 elaborates, "For the LORD will pass through to smite the Egyptians; and when he seeth the blood upon the lintel, and on the two side posts, the LORD will pass over the door, and will not suffer the destroyer to come in unto your houses to smite you."

While Egypt was experiencing the judgment of God, the people of God rested secure. But note that their security rested *in a personal sheltering under the blood of the lamb.* The blood had to be put on every doorpost on every home. Every life was numbered; every individual had to be covered, protected, and made secure by the blood of the lamb. Every member of every family was personally involved. The ultimatum was clear: every person either had to be sheltered under the blood or had to perish. Those were the only choices. The blood was necessary for their protection from God's wrath.

Since all men are sinners, and the wages of sin is death, there must be death in every home, either the death of the firstborn or the death of the slain lamb. God promises his people that he will take the death of the slain lamb as a substitute for the death of the firstborn. That is God's covenant with his people. He calls Israel his *firstborn*, openly inviting them to be sheltered under the blood of the Lamb. The Israelite who chose the blood was delivered, while the one who ignored it was destroyed.

Blood is still necessary today for the forgiveness of sin. It is the way God fulfills this wonderful, vicarious sacrifice in Jesus. For he was wounded for our transgressions and bruised for our iniquities, and he had the chastisement of our peace put upon him (Isa. 53:5).

Judgment falls either on the Lamb of God or on us. God promises that he will receive and honor that substitute, but we must be sheltered by Spirit-worked faith under his blood-bought promise and love. Then Christ's blood will serve both as our propitiation to turn God's wrath from us and as our expiation to cover our sin. Thank God for his Passover Lamb, whose blood is of infinite value to save us.

It is not sufficient to take shelter in a church tradition or a conservative background or a godly upbringing. We must personally flee to the Lamb of God, cast ourselves on his merciful blood, and surrender to its protection. The blood of the Messiah Lamb must be brought by the Holy Spirit to our hearts, then applied to the doorposts of our hearts. Are you sheltered under the blood of the crucified Messiah?

Eating the Supper

Exodus 12 also provides us with details about how the lamb is to be eaten. First, *the lamb must be sacrificed at the appointed time*. We are told in Exodus 12:6 that the congregation of Israel must kill the Passover lamb in the evening, between 3:00 and 6:00 PM. The time is important for two reasons. Christ died on the day of Passover during the very hours when the Passover sacrifices were being offered. At 3:00 PM, Jesus was still alive; at that moment, the ninth hour, he uttered his great cry of dereliction. Also, he was taken down from the cross before 6:00 PM, when the high Sabbath officially began. When the Romans inspected him sometime before 6:00 PM, they found that he had already died. In perfect fulfillment of prophecy, our Lord died on the day of the Passover precisely when the Passover sacrifices were being offered.

Furthermore, we are told in Exodus 12:46 that *not a bone of the Passover lamb could be broken*, either in the slaying or the eating of it. Later on, the psalmist also prophesied that not one of the Messiah's bones should be broken. And John 19:36 tells us that not one bone of Christ was broken, so that we might know that God kept all his bones. This was yet another proof that Jesus is indeed the Passover Lamb of God. Once Christ had cried out on the cross, "It is finished" (John 19:30), ungodly hands could never again touch his body. The enemies' intention to break his bones failed. So did their plan to take Jesus down from the cross and cast his body into a common criminals' pit. God protected his Son, using Nicodemus, Joseph of Arimathea, and even Pilate to arrange for his honorable burial.

Third, *the lamb must be eaten.* Exodus 12:8 specifies, "They shall eat the flesh in that night, roast with fire, and unleavened bread; and with bitter herbs they shall eat it." This refers to roasting, not boiling. Boiling a lamb necessitated a cooking pot, thereby keeping the lamb hidden from view. But roasting took place in the open. In this night of observations, the family gathered around the spit. They watched as flames began to burn into the flesh of the lamb. Juices and blood oozed out, dripping down into the fire.

We are saved by the blood of the Lamb, spiritually speaking, but we must also eat of the Lamb for our nourishment. This speaks of our sanctification, our being set apart for holiness. In its eating, the lamb was to be *wholly consumed*: "Ye shall let nothing of it remain until the morning; and that which remaineth of it until the morning ye shall burn with fire" (Ex. 12:10).

The Passover lamb offered a precious supply that was not to be wasted. Josephus tells us that a lamb could normally feed a household of fourteen people. If a household had only seven people, two households should come together so as not to waste the lamb. The lamb was too precious to be wasted.

Similarly, we are spiritually to take all of Christ today. In the Lord's Supper, we partake of the full Christ, feasting on him and his benefits both mentally and spiritually. In the sacrament as well as in our daily lives, we are to meditate on all aspects of Christ's being. We are to meditate on how he thought; on his hands and how they worked; on his feet and where they went; and on his total body, sanctified for the Father's use. We must pray to be conformed to him, to be wholly sanctified through his truth. We are to feed on his offices, states, and natures—all aspects of him—for the purpose of being sanctified to him, as 1 Thessalonians 5:23 says: "And the very God of peace sanctify you wholly; and I pray God your whole spirit and soul and body be preserved blameless unto the coming of our Lord Jesus Christ."

Additionally, *the lamb was to be eaten with bitter herbs*. The Israelites were to eat the sweet lamb with herbs that were distasteful to the mouth. This also led to sanctification. First, it reminded God's people of the bitterness of their bondage in Egypt, so as to arouse gratitude in their hearts. Second, it taught them self-denial by reminding them of the need for obedience in submitting their will to what is distasteful.

If you give your son a dollar and say, "Buy yourself an ice cream cone," your son learns nothing about obedience, because that is exactly what he wants to do. If, however, you tell your son to do some chore that is not agreeable to him, and he submits his will to yours, he begins to learn obedience. In sanctification, obedience conforms us to Christ, who learned obedience through his suffering. He had to cry out with total submission, "Not my will, but thine, be done" (Luke 22:42). Likewise, as God leads us into distasteful, bitter experiences in daily life, and we submit to his will, we are being sanctified in the footsteps of our Master.

Moreover, in future years when the Passover was commemorated, *the lamb was to be eaten with unleavened bread*. Exodus 12:15–22 repeats the importance of this several times. Unleavened bread supplied the Israelites with two important reminders. First, it reminded them of their hasty departure. Unleavened bread could be made quickly because the dough did not have to rise. This bread was to remind the Israelites, as verses 33–34 indicate, that once they came under the Passover blood of the lamb, they would have to leave Egypt with haste, making no preparation or provision for the new land to which God would lead them.

Secondly, unleavened bread was symbolic of the need for holiness, for it was made of pure wheat without yeast. Yeast symbolized sin because of the way it grows and spreads. As yeast ferments, it works its way through the dough, much like how sin spreads. This served to remind Israel to keep themselves pure from sin, especially from the sins of Egypt. God wanted Israel to make a clean sweep of all Egyptian sinfulness. Symbolically, this means, for us today, that once we come under the Passover blood of Jesus Christ, we are to leave old ways of sin at once; we are to trust God that he will supply all of our needs. We are not to remain in Egypt for the supplying of our needs.

This leads to our sanctification. As we feast on Christ, meditating on him, reading of him, and participating in him by faith, we will be more conformed to his thoughts and will learn to pray more in his name. We will become more Christlike, bearing his fruit. Unleavened bread reminds us that we cannot sustain ourselves in our hasty journey to eternity but are dependent on God to supply all our needs. We are not to tolerate any habit of sin but are to journey on in obedience to our Lord and Master, trusting him for sustenance.

All of this is signified and sealed to us today in the Lord's Supper. The blood of the Lamb speaks of Christ *for* us to save us; the feast of the Lamb speaks of Christ *in* us to sanctify and strengthen us. Both of these truths are brought before us at the Lord's Supper. The Lamb of God is totally sufficient for the people of God. In John 6:55 and 57, Jesus speaks of himself as the one who satisfies the deepest needs of sinners: "For my flesh is meat indeed, and my blood is drink indeed. . . . As the living Father hath sent me, and I live by the Father: so he that eateth me, even he shall live by me." Jesus is telling us that salvation is to be found in him through his broken body and shed blood, but he is also saying that all our sustenance, nourishment, and strength come from the application of his broken body and shed blood to the "doorposts" of our souls.

We come to Communion not only to remind ourselves of where our salvation lies but also to find in Jesus the strength for our weak faith, the satisfaction for which our soul longs, and the quenching of our thirst.

Were it not for Christ, God's judgment would be poised over us to destroy us, but at the Supper we confess that God's judgment has been poured out on Christ so that we may be set free in him and be strengthened by him. In him we find everything—the key to the heart of God, to the reality of salvation—yes, the key to heaven itself. In him our souls delight. We feed on Christ and are satisfied in him. We confess:

> *None but Christ can satisfy;*
> *None other Name for me,*
> *There is love, and life, and lasting joy,*
> *Lord Jesus, found in Thee.*[4]

One last point made in the eating of the Passover lamb is exceedingly precious: *the lamb is to be available to all*. The account of

Passover makes this very clear. Exodus 12:3 says, "They shall take to them every man a lamb." Christ our Passover is available today to all who hear the gospel. The message goes out to all to come to him with the reassurance that those who do come shall in no wise be cast out (John 6:37). "All comers are welcome" as Matthew Henry delighted to say so many times in his famous commentary on the Bible.[5] The blood of Christ is sufficient for everyone who comes; it is sufficient for the need of a thousand worlds. There is infinite fullness in him. Exodus 12 makes it plain that there is no shortage of supply in the Passover lamb. No one who is hungry for the Lamb will be rejected.

Following the Lamb

Exodus 12 also speaks about how God's people were to live. Did you notice God's unique instructions to his people in verse 11? They were to eat at suppertime but be dressed as they would be for breakfast. They were to go out with staff in hand, with loins girded (that is, with long, flowing robes pulled up and tucked under a belt), and shoes on their feet. And they were to eat the Lord's Passover feast in haste. The entire time they were eating this lamb with the unleavened bread and the bitter herbs, they were to remember they were pilgrims en route to the Promised Land.

So God calls us to remember that our citizenship is not here, but in heaven. We are to set our affections on things above, on the heavenly city, which is our heavenly home. We are not to think of ourselves as tourists meandering through life, enjoying everything along the way, but as pilgrims headed for the heavenly land of Canaan with our triune God.

The Passover lamb stands at the end of one life and is the beginning of another, new life. God's goal was to deliver his children from the slavery of Egypt into a new life of pilgrimage. They were committed as God's people from that day on to walking with God with a sense of urgency as they fixed their eyes on the kingdom that God had prepared for them. God would guide them with a pillar of

cloud by day and a pillar of fire by night because the blood of the
lamb had released them and committed them to a pilgrimage all the
way to eternal glory.

So it is with us. God calls us in his Supper to a life of new obedience, new trust, and new devotion until the day when the redeemed
will forever sing in glory at the marriage feast of the Lamb:

> *Worthy is the Lamb that was slain*
> *To receive power, and riches, and wisdom, and strength, and*
> *honour, and glory, and blessing.* (Rev. 5:12)

As we taste and handle the bread and the wine of the Lord's
Supper, we do so as a foretaste of that infinite glory, asking God to
send us forth, living on Christ and living for Christ. Then, when we
reach the marriage supper of the Lamb, we will enter into a glory
that we have already begun to taste here below.

On the other hand, the eternal fruit of the Lamb signals the destruction of all those who do not shelter under his blood. They will perish
forever, just as the Egyptians perished. We read that "at midnight the
LORD smote all the firstborn in the land of Egypt" (Ex. 12:29). How
unexpected! Egypt went to bed that night as usual, once more ignoring
God's warnings. But suddenly, "at midnight the LORD smote."

Will this be your experience when God's final judgment comes?
If you are not sheltered under Christ's blood, the time will still come
when God will take you to eternity. You will go to sleep as usual but
will wake up in eternity.

A Picture of Judgment

At midnight, we look out over Egypt. It is darkness; there is no light
anywhere; everyone is fast asleep. Suddenly, on the horizon we see
a bright light descend from heaven, a destroying angel sent to pass
through Egypt. We see the angel pausing at every house for just a
moment, moving swiftly through, as Peter says, "as a thief in the
night" (2 Pet. 3:10). Are you ready for that angel of death? Are you

prepared? Or is death going to be the greatest shock of your life? In the darkness of midnight, the Lord smites all those who are not sheltering under the blood of Christ.

What destruction there was in Egypt that night! Exodus 12:29 says, "The LORD smote all the firstborn in the land of Egypt, from the firstborn of Pharaoh that sat on his throne unto the firstborn of the captive that was in the dungeon; and all the firstborn of cattle." Imagine a wife awakening suddenly, hearing a groan. She turns and watches her husband, who is a firstborn, die. She runs to the bedroom to wake up her children, and one doesn't stir. He is gone as well. Then she runs outside and sees neighbors coming out of their homes, weeping. "My son is gone; my husband is dead!" Tens of thousands of people are slain. What destruction!

There is worse to come. At the final judgment, not only the firstborn need worry but also the second, and the third—all who are born. From the oldest to the youngest, none are excluded. What destruction will come on anyone who is not sheltered under the blood of Christ. What astounding judgment!

Notice also that it is a *very determined judgment*. God said: "For I will pass through the land of Egypt this night, and will smite all the firstborn in the land of Egypt, both man and beast; and against all the gods of Egypt I will execute judgment: I am the LORD" (Ex. 12:12). There is sheer, unstoppable determination here. Nothing can keep out this destroying angel. Maybe some who heard the warning took some action. Maybe they put extra locks on the door or nailed it shut, but what good would that do? Nothing could keep out this destroying angel—nothing but blood. Where there was blood, there was complete safety, even life in the midst of death. Nothing could get over that threshold. God would keep his promises.

Remember, this is only a picture. But put yourself in the picture. Live as an Egyptian for a moment or two. Try to hear the cries. Try to hear the desolation, the despair. Can you hear it? There is death of the firstborn in every family and even in every barn, among the precious livestock. There is wailing and mourning and rending of garments everywhere.

But how different it was for God's people! In Numbers 33:3–4 we are told how the children of Israel left Egypt: "On the morrow after the passover the children of Israel went out with an high hand in the sight of all the Egyptians. For the Egyptians buried all their firstborn, which the LORD had smitten among them: upon their gods also the LORD executed judgments." The blood-bought people are leaving their houses with a high hand, while the Egyptians line the streets with the dead in their hands. Is this not a remarkable, predictive picture of final judgment, when the Lord will separate the sheep from the goats?

When he says to the goats, "Depart from me, ye cursed" and to the sheep, "Come, ye blessed of my Father, inherit the kingdom prepared for you from the foundation of the world" (Matt. 25:41, 34), what side will you be on? Will you find yourself, like the Egyptians, with death in your arms? Or will you find yourself going out of this world to eternity with a high hand, saved and delivered by the blood of the Lamb? Where will you be: on the side of mourning or the side of rejoicing?

How vital it is that you would look on the cross of Christ and its shed blood and say, "That is what I need. I need a sacrifice, a substitute, a Savior. I need Christ. His blood is my only hope. That is all I cover myself with; I do not add my good works, my law keeping, or anything I have ever accomplished. He alone is my only hope. Only when God sees the blood will he pass over me."

You may ask, was it fair of God to punish the Egyptians? But of course the Egyptians deserved to perish. They mistreated God's people. They rejected God's Word. They ignored the plagues. They were repeatedly warned in vain. Justice slew the firstborn of Egypt; mercy saved the children of Israel.

The final judgment will be the same. People here may protest the final judgment, saying, "Hell is too great a punishment. It is not fair; it is too unending. God is not fair or just." Can you hear these devilish whispers in your heart? When you think of hell and of eternity, do these thoughts rise up? "I don't like it, I don't want it; I don't believe it. That is not my God." Well, if he is not your God, then, as someone once said, "prepare to meet a stranger, and prepare to meet appropriate judgment."

Have you not mistreated God's people? Have you not rejected God's work? Have you not ignored invitation after invitation, blessing after blessing, and warning after warning throughout your life? Has he not come to you in one more plague, one more hard providence, one more bereavement, one more disappointment, one more frustration, one more family hardship, one more loss of a job, one more episode of ill health? Do you really think, in the light of all God has given to you and done for you and shown to you—in the light of all you have rejected and ignored—that you will stand before him and say, "This judgment is not fair"?

If that great day finds us on the side of the mourning, the judgment will be only appropriate. It will be our own fault for refusing to take shelter behind the blood of Christ.

Still Avoidable

Happily, a final observation from the Passover story reminds us that while the final judgment will be astounding and appropriate, it is still avoidable now.

Pharaoh and his servants eventually took action. Exodus 12:31 says that Pharaoh called for Moses and Aaron by night—even before they came to him—but it was too late. Had Pharaoh and his people repented earlier and found shelter behind the blood of the lamb, they would have found mercy; but now judgment has fallen.

This begs a necessary question: are you sheltered in the blood of the Lamb of God's provision? Do you possess, by faith, the passport of Christ's blood, the only way to enter into heaven? Are you ready for God's coming judgment? Do you have the Lamb of God's provision to present to God?

It is not enough to know that a Savior is provided for us. If you would be saved from God's wrath to come and live in the freedom and safety of God's people, it is necessary for you to trust in Christ as the necessary Lamb God has provided, as the necessary sacrifice ordered according to God's command, and as the necessary and only place of refuge. If you do not exercise faith in Christ's blood—if the blood of Christ is not sprinkled on the posts of your heart—although you might know that Christ died for sinners, it will do you no good. You must take shelter beneath the blood of Christ. You must by faith place the blood of Christ between the holy God of Israel and your own sins. The blood of Christ is absolutely necessary; it had to be shed, it must be applied, it must be received. Fly to it today. Take refuge in Christ's blood or perish forever.

REDEEMING BLOOD

W. Robert Godfrey

Like sheep they are appointed for Sheol;
death shall be their shepherd,
and the upright shall rule over them in the morning.
Their form shall be consumed in Sheol, with no
place to dwell.
But God will ransom my soul from the power of Sheol,
for he will receive me.

—Psalm 49:14–15

We go to very great lengths to avoid having to face the reality of death. Have you noticed the careful euphemisms that we use? We seldom hear anymore that anyone dies. People pass on—an interesting euphemism originally coined presumably by Christian Scientists, who deny the reality of death. You just pass on; you don't die. Christian Scientists had a terrible time when Franklin Delano Roosevelt died. What headline should be in *The Christian Scientist Monitor*? Perhaps "Truman Becomes President."

Death Avoided?

Even Christians are sometimes guilty of such avoidance. Upon a person's death it is often heard, "He went home." This is a biblical notion, of course, and should not be attacked, but it can be a euphemism that we use to avoid having to face the reality of the solemnity, the finality of death. Sometimes we might even say, "We lost someone." Oscar Wilde had a wonderful comment on this saying. His prospective mother-in-law asked him about his parents, and he said, "I've lost them." She responded, "Well losing one parent is understandable, but losing two seems careless." So there is this determined effort to avoid facing death. This has been a fairly long-standing problem in America.

Sixty years ago the great English novelist Evelyn Waugh wrote a masterpiece comic novel about funeral practices in Southern California, entitled *The Loved One*. He describes funerals at the great cemetery in Southern California. He changes its name, but it is clearly Forest Lawn. The viewing rooms for mourners of corpses is called the Slumber Room. The deceased are always referred to as the loved ones, and they are laid out in appropriate poses as if they are sleeping and, as much as possible, in other familiar poses. One woman was laid out holding a telephone. All of that is done for the purpose of trying to avoid facing the reality of death.

Aimee Semple McPherson was a Pentecostal preacher and healer and probably the most famous woman in America in the 1920s and 1930s. She was invited to speak to the atheist society at the University of Glasgow. She was willing to preach anywhere, so she arrived upon a platform that was littered with cigar butts, cigarette butts, and empty beer bottles. As she came out on the platform, the atheists hooted and hollered and carried on, but Aimee just stood there calmly. When they finally settled down, she leaned over and said, "Can I tell you a story? It's about an atheist. He died you know, and they laid him out in a coffin. Oh, he looked fine. They laid him out so nice, all dressed up, all made up, and looking marvelous. A friend came by, looked in the coffin, and said 'oh, he looks fine.' Oh, he looked fine, but he is an atheist. He doesn't believe in Heaven. He doesn't believe in Hell. All dressed up and nowhere to go."

The psalmist, in Psalm 49, did what Aimee did, only in a much more serious manner. Aimee forced these atheists to come back to think about the great reality that life ends. We do not live in this world forever. We do not live in this body forever. What does that mean about understanding the meaning of life? What does that make us think about as we ponder the future? How does that affect our values and our way of valuing and understanding this life?

Death, the Great Equalizer

Psalm 49 is fascinating because it is not addressed to Israel, as most of the psalms are. It's not addressed to God's people, but to the whole world. "Hear this, all peoples! . . . My mouth shall speak wisdom" (Ps. 49:1, 3). When we face this universal reality that we will all die, we need wisdom to understand what that means and how it affects the way we should live. This is what this psalm wants to direct us to.

The psalm is written out of a very particular frustration on the part of the psalmist, that the rich seem always to be cheating the poor. He is frustrated by the apparent lack of justice and fairness in this world. He meditates on how we should understand life in light of that unfairness and comes to an arresting conclusion. Death is the great equalizer: both the rich and the poor alike die, both the wise and the foolish alike die, both the righteous and the wicked alike die. They don't simply pass on; they die.

In magnificently beautiful, poetical language, Psalm 49 talks about what death is all about. "Their graves are their homes forever, their dwelling places to all generations, though they called lands by their own names" (v. 11). Even the rich who are powerful enough to conquer lands and give those lands their own names—they die like everybody else. Even those who can build splendid monuments in which to have themselves buried—even if it's pyramids four thousand years old in Egypt—they are forever their homes. For as verse 14 says, "Like sheep they are appointed for Sheol; death shall be their shepherd." Death shall be their shepherd. Moreover, "Their form shall be consumed in Sheol, with no place to dwell."

This is very solemn, isn't it? Do you notice this is a psalm written by the sons of Korah? It must have been an interesting family to be part of, Korah's family. Korah was the man who rebelled against Moses during the exodus and was swallowed by the ground as God's judgment (see Numbers 16). How that story must have been told from generation to generation about Korah and his faith, and how Korah went down alive to Sheol for his disobedience of the Lord. These verses must have echoed in the mind of the sons of Korah as they wrote that their forebearer, in his defiance of God, had gone down alive into that netherworld to live forever and never see the light.

No Avoidance

What conclusion does the psalmist draw from this meditation? At first glance, it would seem to be the rather stoic conclusion that his oppressors die and we die: *we are all going to die, so get over it.* Of course, that is not the ultimate conclusion of the psalm. But the psalmist, in meditating on death, wants to press our human helplessness in the face of death. Think of verses 7 to 9: "Truly no man can ransom another, or give to God the price of his life, for the ransom of their life is costly and can never suffice, that he should live on forever and never see the pit." We can uncomfortably be forced to think about the fact that no matter how rich a person might be, the richest among us don't have enough money to prevent the death of one we love when death comes as the shepherd. No ransom can be paid nor is there any sufficient price. All will go down to death.

With that reality the psalmist wants to shake us and force us not to avoid death. The death rate is 100 percent, given enough time. This psalm wants us to come face-to-face with that and only then to turn to its own glorious confession of faith, "But God will ransom my soul" (v. 15). The most powerful, the most wealthy, the most glorious in human history are all powerless before the face of death. But what no human being can do, God can do. That is what this psalm wants to remind us. That is the essential wisdom that this psalm would teach us: God is not defeated by death.

Israel's Deliverance

Psalm 49 includes a refrain that it develops and uses for its conclusion. Verse 12 introduces "man in his pomp." This is the psalm's special target: man in all the splendor that he can gather to himself, all the velvet and ermine and gold that he can wear. The psalmist declares of him, "Man in his pomp will not remain; he is like the beasts that perish." If we were doing a modern translation, we might render this: "You'll die like a dog." The psalm concludes by coming back to this theme: "Man in his pomp yet without understanding is like the beasts that perish" (Ps. 49:20).

The last word of God is not that man with his pomp will die like the beasts. The last word is that "man will die like the beasts *if he lacks understanding*"— if he lacks wisdom, if he lacks insight into the essential truth. The essential truth is that God can ransom a soul. God can keep us from the power of Sheol and will receive us to himself. When the Israelites of old read that verse, the word *ransom* or *redemption*—the idea of being delivered and rescued and particularly bought back—would have resonated with them. They would have remembered their own history. They would have remembered the laws under which they lived, because their history and laws were filled with the language and thought of redemption, of ransom.

Think of these words that reflect on Israel's deliverance from Egypt: "The Lord set his love on you and chose you . . . it is because the Lord loves you and is keeping the oath that he swore to your fathers, that the Lord has brought you out with a mighty hand and redeemed you from the house of slavery, from the hand of Pharaoh king of Egypt" (Deut. 7:7–8). Israel was bought with a price and brought forth from Egypt—rescued, delivered, ransomed. That same language is to be found in the prophet Isaiah as he reflects on Israel being gathered back from exile: "And a highway shall be there, and it shall be called the Way of Holiness. . . . No lion shall be there, nor shall any ravenous beast come up on it; they shall not be found there, but the redeemed shall walk there. And the ransomed of the LORD shall return and come to Zion with singing" (Isa. 35:8–10).

Ransomed

So from the beginning of Israel's national history to the promise of its recovery, the language is that of redemption, of ransom from the hand of God. God not only wanted Israel to remember that history and that promise, but God also wanted Israel to be embraced by that reality in every moment of its living. The law is full of this language as well, the law that so often we skip over quickly when we read through the five books of Moses. Consider, for example in Exodus 21:28–30, what happens when an ox gores a neighbor:

> "When an ox gores a man or woman to death, the ox shall be stoned, and its flesh shall not be eaten, but the owner of the ox shall not be liable. But if the ox has been accustomed to gore in the past, and its owner has been warned but has not kept it in, and it kills a man or a woman, the ox shall be stoned, and its owner also shall be put to death. If a ransom is imposed on him, then he shall give for the redemption of his life whatever is imposed on him."

God reminds his people that when the law is violated, the only hope is that some ransom might be paid to deliver the transgressor from the penalty of the law. For some crimes there was no ransom. About murder, we read in Numbers:

> "If anyone kills a person, the murderer shall be put to death on the evidence of witnesses. But no person shall be put to death on the testimony of one witness. Moreover, you shall accept no ransom for the life of a murderer, who is guilty of death, but he shall be put to death. And you shall accept no ransom for him who has fled to his city of refuge, that he may return to dwell in the land

before the death of the high priest. You shall not pollute the land in which you live, for blood pollutes the land, and no atonement can be made for the land for the blood that is shed in it, except by the blood of the one who shed it. You shall not defile the land in which you live, in the midst of which I dwell, for I the LORD dwell in the midst of the people of Israel." (Num. 35:30–34)

Again, in relation to slavery, we read: "If your brother, a Hebrew man or a Hebrew woman, is sold to you, he shall serve you six years, and in the seventh year you shall let him go free from you. . . . You shall remember that you were a slave in the land of Egypt, and the LORD your God redeemed you; therefore I command you this today" (Deut. 15:12, 15). At every point, Israel had laws that spoke of redemption and ransom, and all of that speaking was intended to remind them that God had ransomed them from Egypt. God had redeemed them. They were never to forget that they were a redeemed people, a ransomed people.

The Firstborn

Very striking is the law of redemption relative to the birth of the firstborn:

> "Every firstborn of a donkey you shall redeem with a lamb, or if you will not redeem it you shall break its neck. Every firstborn of man among your sons you shall redeem. And when in time to come your son asks you, 'What does this mean?' you shall say to him, 'By a strong hand the LORD brought us out of Egypt, from the house of slavery. For when Pharaoh stubbornly refused to let us go, the LORD killed all the firstborn in the land of Egypt, both the firstborn of man and the firstborn of animals. Therefore I sacrifice to the LORD all the males that first open the womb, but all the firstborn of my sons I redeem.'" (Ex. 13:13–15)

Every time there was a firstborn in the house of Israel, they were to redeem that firstborn, thus remembering how the Lord had redeemed them from Egypt at the price of Egypt's firstborn.

Sometimes I suspect some of us have thought that maybe God was a little hard on the firstborn. Why the firstborn of Egypt? But God explains. If we listen carefully enough, there is almost always a reason for what God does. God sent Moses with this explanation: "Then you shall say to Pharaoh, 'Thus says the LORD, Israel is my firstborn son, and I say to you, "Let my son go that he may serve me." If you refuse to let him go, behold, I will kill your firstborn son'" (Ex. 4:22–23).

Pharaoh, forgetful of all that Joseph had done for Egypt to save them from starvation, had enslaved Joseph's sons, but they were not just Joseph's sons; they were God's firstborn as his people. God's warning to Pharaoh went something like this: "If you try to destroy my firstborn in slavery, then I will destroy your firstborn. I will redeem my people at the cost of your firstborn Egypt. I will display my power over the gods of Egypt. I will drown your living god in the Red Sea. I will kill the firstborn of your families and of your animals to display that I am the Lord." But Pharaoh hardened his heart. Though he was warned again and again, at last God's judgment came, and Israel was redeemed. God's people were redeemed out of the house of bondage at the cost of Egypt's firstborn.

Life through the Blood

The picture of redemption throughout the Old Testament is a picture of life coming out of death at the cost of death, life as being bought by a substitute who dies. That is the picture painted over and over in so many marvelous ways in the Old Testament. One of the striking testimonies of the truthfulness of the Bible as God's revelation is its coherence. Authors separated by centuries of history and remarkably different cultures are all saying fundamentally the same message: God alone brings life to people caught up in death, and God alone brings life through a ransom paid, a ransom paid by a substitute so that the one whom God is bringing to life might live.

This shows that the whole Old Testament is really a preparation for us to understand the work of Jesus Christ. Israel is God's firstborn only in a preparatory sense because the true firstborn of God is Jesus Christ. Likewise, Israel's sacrifices are only preparatory sacrifices. The New Testament makes this abundantly clear. The blood of bulls and goats can never take away sin but was a preparation (cf. Heb. 10:1–4).

The sacrificed bulls and goats were to prepare our minds to understand the work of Jesus Christ. If there had been no Old Testament in existence when Jesus came into the world, and John the Baptist had still said, "Behold, the Lamb of God, who takes away the sin of the world!" (John 1:29), nobody would have had a clue what John was talking about. His audience knew what a lamb was and the function of lambs in the sacrificial system of Israel. They knew that a lamb slain took away sin. So when John the Baptist gave his testimony about the Savior, it was like a lightning bolt of clarity.

The Old Testament was about Jesus Christ; it pointed to him and his coming. He is the Lamb, he is the substitute, he is the ransom, and he is the redemption. Through his blood Christ takes away the sin of the world—blood, because the life is in the blood. And when he pours out his blood, he is pouring out his life unto death, that everyone who is found in him might live. That is a promise, as he is the firstborn. Colossians 1:18 says: "He is the head of the body, the church. He is the beginning, the firstborn from the dead, that in everything he might be preeminent." And Romans 8:29 adds that we are predestined to salvation so that Jesus "might be the firstborn among many brothers." That is what the death of Jesus Christ and his glorious resurrection are all about, that he might be the firstborn of those who are in him so that they will have life and deliverance. God will ransom souls in the redemption of his Son, in the blood of his Son, and in the death and resurrection of his Son.

Redemption for Every Sin

Paul wrote so gloriously in 2 Timothy 1:10 about "the appearing of our Savior Christ Jesus, who abolished death and brought life and immortality to light through the gospel." But for whom did Jesus abolish death? Does this mean that nobody has to read or worry about Psalm 49 anymore? No, that is not the message of the Scripture. Instead, the message is that Christ abolished death for everyone who knows him and is in him, everyone who accepts him and trusts him. The glory of the gospel message is that there is no sin that the blood of Jesus Christ cannot cover. We read in the law that murderers in Israel could not be redeemed, because the land had to be purified. But the glorious message of the gospel declares there is no sin so terrible that it cannot be redeemed in the blood of Jesus Christ.

How important it is for the church to bear this message of forgiveness into this world! There are people with a very sensitive conscience who may reflect upon their life and think, "The blood of Jesus Christ may cover other people's sins, but it couldn't cover mine." But it can. The blood of Christ will cover your sins if you turn to him and ask.

The Devil tells us a great lie when he comes to us and says, "God won't forgive that." Don't forget that the Hebrew name *Satan* means "Accuser." The Devil has two accusing functions. He accuses God to us: "God's not reliable, God's not really there, God won't keep his promises." But he also accuses us before God and impresses on our conscience that God will never receive us, never accept us, and never forgive us. But the truth of the gospel is that the blood of Jesus Christ will cover every sin.

This is why the word of the prophet Ezekiel cries out to every one of us: "I have no pleasure in the death of the wicked, but that the wicked turn from his way and live; turn back, turn back from your evil ways, for why will you die, O house of Israel?" (Ezek. 33:11). There is an abundance of mercy and compassion in Jesus Christ. There is an abundance of life in Jesus Christ. Why would you choose death? Why would you follow the shepherd death into Sheol where there is only darkness and gnashing of teeth? For the Lord of Life comes to you in his Word and says, "Come to me, all who labor and are heavy laden, and I will give you rest" (Matt. 11:28).

God's Word of Redemption

Many commentators believe that, to some extent, the story of the rich man and Lazarus in Luke 16 echoes themes found in Psalm 49. The rich man is in Sheol. He either had not read Psalm 49 or had not taken it to heart, for he is now in deep agony, separated from God and his mercy. He pleads for just a little water to mitigate his suffering, and there is no water. Then he pleads, "Send back Lazarus to warn my brothers. Surely," he says, "they will listen if a man rises from the dead" (cf. Luke 16:27–30). What remarkable words! His brothers had all the evidence they needed in just considering the order of the universe that God made.

God did bring Jesus back to life to testify to life and establish a people of life to go into the world preaching the gift of life in the blood of Jesus Christ. But who has believed our report? Listen to Abraham's answer to rich Lazarus's request: "If they do not hear Moses and the Prophets, neither will they be convinced if someone should rise from the dead" (Luke 16:31). They don't really need a man to come back from the dead, because they have Moses in the Scriptures. Let them listen to him. It is almost as if Abraham is saying, "Let them listen to Psalm 49!"

Psalm 49 won't let us get away from the reality of death as the universal human experience, and the only hope, the only antidote, the only deliverance is to be found in the God who ransoms us by the costly blood of his own well-beloved Son. If God has left a testimony to himself in the world that he made, a testimony clear and shining in the Word that he inspired, and a testimony in the Son that he raised from the dead, and if God has raised a testimony in his church of people who have been brought from death to life, what more exactly could he do?

But some will say, "If only I could see those miracles that are recorded in the New Testament, if only I could see them for myself." But what happened to the majority of people who did see those miracles in their day? They still managed to turn away and suppress the truth in unrighteousness. They still managed to think only about themselves and not about the Christ. The miracles were intended to draw their minds to Christ—his glory, his love, his mercy, and his kindness. God gave the most valuable gift he had, his own Son, for our redemption. What will God make, then, of those who trample the blood of the Son under their feet, despise the blood of the covenant, and insist on their own wisdom?

Psalm 49:13 gives an answer: "This is the path of those who have foolish confidence; yet after them people approve of their boasts." People approve of what the world says. The wisdom of the world is what many insist on following, but the wisdom of the world leads to death. The wisdom of God leads to life through the extravagant work of Jesus Christ the firstborn Son.

The judgment that fell on Pharaoh's son and Egypt's sons—that curse with its dereliction and destruction—God turned and placed on his Son for the redemption of his people. If that does not move our hearts in the love of God for sinners, what more can be said? "Do not let death be your shepherd," the psalm instructs, but find in Jesus Christ the Good Shepherd who gave his life for the sheep and who promises to lead us by still waters and in green pastures and to deliver our souls and give us life—abundant life now and a glorious life beyond our imagination—in a new heaven and a new earth in which righteousness dwells forever.

ATONING BLOOD

Philip Graham Ryken

For all have sinned and fall short of the glory of God, and are justified by his grace as a gift, through the redemption that is in Christ Jesus, whom God put forward as a propitiation by his blood, to be received by faith. This was to show God's righteousness, because in his divine forbearance he had passed over former sins.

—Romans 3:23–25

In producing his famous translation of the Bible, the English Reformer William Tyndale introduced many memorable words and phrases into the English language. Ultimately these words came from the Holy Spirit, of course, but someone still had to decide how the divine words of the Old and New Testaments should be translated from Hebrew and Greek into English. The Bible that resulted from Tyndale's work is full of memorable phrases that have become everyday expressions: "let there be light"; "the salt of the earth"; "the spirit is willing"; "the powers that be"; and so on.

In addition to his special gift for the rhythms of language, Tyndale also had a passion for choosing the best words to communicate biblical truth. For this reason he invented several important words related to salvation, including *Passover*, *scapegoat*, and *atonement*.

Tyndale's use of the term *atonement* began with the recognition that no single word in the English language fully did justice to Christ's saving work on the cross. The word *reconciliation* came close, in his view, yet it only expressed the restored relationship that resulted from the work of Christ without really saying anything about *how* Jesus dealt with the problem of sin. Tyndale wanted a word that would express *both* the remission of our sin *and* our reconciliation to God. Since there was no such word in the English language, Tyndale decided to make up a new one, much the way that the apostle Paul invented new terms to express theological truth.[1]

The word Tyndale decided to use was *atonement*, or "at-one-ment" (e.g., Num. 6:11; 2 Cor. 5:18). Taken literally, *atonement* is really just another word for reconciliation, for two becoming one. But because it was a new term, it was able to take on new meaning. Atonement quickly became a basic theological term for the sacrifice of Christ on the cross, which makes us right with God by satisfying the claims of divine justice. Thus *atonement* satisfied Tyndale's desire to express both the relationship we have with God and the way Christ died to save us.

The Centrality of the Atonement

Doubtless Tyndale would be pleased to know that today the primary meaning of *atonement* in the English dictionary is "the reconciliation of God and man through the sacrificial death of Jesus Christ."[2] But he would be much less pleased to know how unpopular atonement has become. Doubtless this is because it deals with too many subjects that most people would rather ignore, like the wrath and curse of God, the punishment of sin, and the old, blood-stained cross. As the Dutch theologian G. C. Berkouwer once explained, "Terms common to jurisprudence have been used in connection with Christ's death: satisfaction, sufficiency, payment, purchase, ransom, and punishment. And these terms have made men angry."[3]

What makes people so reluctant to embrace the death of Jesus as the atonement for their sins? Most unbelievers do not see their need for atonement. "Why would anyone else have to die for my sins?" they ask. For their part, many Christians do not understand the meaning of the atonement. The notion of a blood sacrifice for sin sounds primitive, perhaps even barbaric. As a result, the cruciality of the cross has all but disappeared from contemporary theology.

One notable example of the many recent attacks on the doctrine of the atonement is an anthology entitled *Stricken by God? Nonviolent Identification and the Victory of Christ.* By and large, the contributors—all of them theologians in the church—do not believe that the cross of Christ saves us through its being the punishment of sin or the satisfaction of the wrath of God. According to the editors, what we need instead is "to construct a new paradigm of the atonement in the 21st century; the sacrificial model is flawed."[4] Fundamental to this new paradigm is the conviction, which the editors identify as a core belief, that "on the Cross, God was not punishing Jesus."[5] To believe otherwise, they say, is the moral equivalent of the mass murderer who slaughtered Amish children at a Pennsylvania schoolhouse.[6]

The orthodox doctrine of the atonement has not always been treated this way. Back in the nineteenth century, in his definitive work on the subject, the great Scottish theologian George Smeaton identified the atonement as "the central truth of Christianity, and the great theme of Scripture."[7] Another Scottish divine wrote:

> Let a man preach with the greatest ability and zeal everything in the Bible but the Cross, he shall, as to the great end of preaching, preach in vain. . . . The doctrine of the atonement ought not to be the sole theme of the Christian ministry, but every doctrine, and every precept, of Christianity should be exhibited in their connection with this great master principle; and the leading object of the preacher should be to keep the mind and the heart of his hearers steadily fixed on Christ Jesus—Christ Jesus crucified.[8]

The Necessity of the Atonement

If ever a theologian kept his mind and heart fixed on Christ crucified it was the apostle Paul. One of the best places to see his doctrine of the atoning blood of Jesus Christ is the third chapter of Romans. Here we see, first of all, and as clearly as anywhere in Scripture, the necessity of the atonement.

A full understanding of the atoning work of Jesus Christ—specifically the blood atonement of his sacrifice on the cross—always begins with the problem of our sin. As Donald Macleod has written, "All shallow views of the atonement are the consequence of shallow perception of sin and superficial awareness of spiritual need. If we know something of the depth of our own depravity and the extent of our own guilt we shall readily appreciate God's provision in the blood of His Son."[9]

This is exactly the approach that Paul takes in Romans. Before showing us God's provision in the blood of his Son, the apostle shows us the depths of our depravity and the extent of our guilt. For nearly two chapters, he explains how "the wrath of God is revealed from heaven against all ungodliness and unrighteousness of men" (Rom. 1:18). No one can escape divine condemnation—not the pagan who tries to ignore the existence of God, not the moral person who tries to lead a good life, and not the religious person who claims to know God. Whether we are Jews or Gentiles, we are all guilty before God. This is true of every person we know in every family, from every neighborhood, in every workplace, and at every church. We are all sinners. To use another one of Tyndale's famous expressions—one that we find in Romans—people have become "a law unto themselves" (Rom. 2:14 KJV).

To prove this point, in chapter 3 Paul piles up passage after passage from the psalms to show that "none is righteous, no, not one; no one understands; no one seeks for God. All have turned aside; together they have become worthless; no one does good, not even one" (Rom. 3:10–12). The language here is categorical: everyone who belongs to the category of mere human being is a fallen sinner. "For all have sinned," Paul goes on to say in verse 23, "and fall short of the glory of God."

We ourselves are part of the problem. This point is so obvious, and the evidence for it so abundant, that it hardly needs a defense. But consider a gentle reminder; for the purpose of self-examination, consider a series of spiritual questions from an old Puritan—questions that test whether we are leading the life that God wants us to live:

- Have I been fervent in prayer?

- Have I practiced God's presence, at least every hour?

- Have I, before every deliberate action or conversation, considered how it might be turned to God's glory?

- Have I sought to center conversations on the other person's interests and needs and ultimately toward God, or did I turn it toward my own interests?

- Have I given thanks to God after every pleasant occurrence or time?

- Have I thought or spoken unkindly of anyone?

- Have I been careful to avoid proud thoughts or comparing myself to others?

- Have I been impure in my thoughts or glances?

- Have I over or under eaten, slept, worked?

- Have I been leading in my home, or only reacting to situations?[10]

If we are honest, when we ask ourselves these questions we quickly realize our sin. We should also realize that there is nothing we can say in our defense. When we hear the law of God, every single commandment is an accusation against us: "Whatever the law says it speaks to those who are under the law, so that every mouth may be stopped, and the whole world may be held accountable to God.

For by works of the law no human being will be justified in his sight, since through the law comes knowledge of sin" (Rom. 3:19–20). This is not a trial in which we are innocent until proven guilty; instead, it is a trial in which we have already been proven guilty and must remain guilty until we are declared righteous.

This is a real problem for us because the wages of sin really is death. It has been that way since the first sin, when God told our first parents that if they sinned, they would die (Gen. 2:17). Thus, by the disobedience of Adam, the entire human race is guilty of sin and doomed to die. As Paul writes later in Romans: "Sin came into the world through one man, and death through sin, and so death spread to all men" (Rom. 5:12). Or again, as the climax to his argument: "The wages of sin is death" (Rom. 6:23).

In order for us to find atonement, therefore, something has to be done about the problem of sin and guilt and death. Anselm of Canterbury learned this in writing his famous book on the atonement, *Cur Deus Homo?* "I came as a sinner to be reconciled," he wrote, but "I find that I am a dead man to be raised."[11]

Atonement by Redemption

Thankfully, the book of Romans is not just about the problem of sin and death, but also about God's solution to our problem in Jesus Christ. Yes, the wages of sin is death, but, as Paul goes on to say, "the free gift of God is eternal life in Christ Jesus our Lord" (Rom. 6:23).

This saving grace comes as a gift. God intervenes in the history of fallen humanity to provide a new and free way of salvation. The provision of that gift is marked by the adversative "But now." To quote Paul's fuller argument:

> But now the righteousness of God has been manifested apart from the law, although the Law and the Prophets bear witness to it— the righteousness of God through faith in Jesus Christ for all who believe. For there is no distinction: for all have sinned and fall

short of the glory of God, and are justified by his grace as a gift, through the redemption that is in Christ Jesus, whom God put forward as a propitiation by his blood, to be received by faith. (Rom. 3:21–25)

Notice again the universal problem of sin: all of us fall short of the glory of God. Notice as well the language of presentation. The righteousness of God is offered to sinners as a gracious gift. But notice especially three vocabulary words that the apostle uses to define and describe our salvation—the doctrines of the atonement.

First there is the word *redemption*—a term for atonement that comes from the marketplace. *Redemption* refers to the procurement of a release through the payment of a price. The word is a commercial term that describes salvation as a business transaction. In fact, some of the common biblical words for redemption (*agorazo, exagorazo*) are derived from the Greek word for an open marketplace (*agora*), where a variety of goods was sold. Probably the most dramatic example of redemption from the ancient world was the price paid for the manumission of a slave. A slave would be offered for sale in the city marketplace, where anyone who was willing to pay the price could purchase the slave's freedom.

When the New Testament talks about redemption, the emphasis almost always falls on the costliness of the price. Here in Romans 3, where redemption is described as a gift, it becomes apparent that the price of that gift is paid in blood. We are redeemed from our bondage to sin through the cross, where Jesus offered his blood as the payment for our sin.

In any redemption, it is necessary for the payment to be made in full. My wife, Lisa, and I learned this during the first months of our marriage. We had very little money to spend on anything extra in those days, so we were delighted to get a cereal box with a coupon for an ice cream Blizzard at Dairy Queen. Carefully we cut the coupon from the box, walked downtown, and presented it for redemption. The server at the window studied our coupon disdainfully and then pronounced, "We don't make that size!" Not having enough money to buy a Blizzard, we sadly walked away.

Praise God that Jesus paid the full price for our redemption! Here is a unique claim in the history of religion. What other deity has ever offered his own blood for the salvation of his people? Only the Redeemer, Jesus Christ. Never discount the cost of salvation. The grace of God did not come cheap. We were "bought with a price" (1 Cor. 6:20): the blood of the Savior who "ransomed people for God" (Rev. 5:9). In the words of an old Easter hymn by Cecil Frances Alexander, "There was no other good enough to pay the price of sin; He only could unlock the gate of heaven, and let us in."[12]

Atonement by Justification

Redemption is not the only aspect of salvation in Romans 3, however. There is also *justification*—a term for atonement that comes from a court of law. Reformation Christianity is sometimes criticized for focusing too much on the doctrine of justification by faith. Yet this is one of the main doctrinal themes of the New Testament, where the vocabulary of justification occurs more than two hundred times, including in this passage. Not only are we redeemed from sin, but we are also "justified by his grace as a gift" (Rom. 3:24).

The mention of grace indicates that justification is more than we deserve. It is an act of God's unmerited favor. As the English Reformer Thomas Cranmer wrote in his *Homily on Salvation*, "No man can, by his own deeds, be justified and made righteous before God: but every man, of necessity, is constrained to seek for another righteousness or justification, to be received at God's own hands."[13] In justification this need is satisfied, for as the Scripture says, "It is God who justifies" (Rom. 8:33).

Justification is a legal declaration of righteousness. It does not make someone righteous but proclaims that someone is righteous with respect to the law. One way to see this is by comparing justification to another declaration that is made in a court of law, namely, the declaration of condemnation. When a judge condemns a man, he does not make the man a criminal but declares him to be a criminal. So also to justify is not to make righteous but to declare righteous.

What is unusual in this case, however, is that the people declared righteous are actually sinners. It is the *ungodly* who are justified—those who are guilty of sin and condemned to die. So on what legal basis does God grant the gift of his righteousness? Since justification comes from the court, it must be established in law. It would be an outrage for a righteous God simply to overlook or to excuse sin. If he intends to justify sinners, he must have some legitimate judicial basis for doing so. Only in this way can he remain just while at the same time justifying sinners (Rom. 3:26).

The way God justifies sinners is on the basis of the perfect life and sacrificial death of Jesus Christ: "When God justifies sinners, he is not declaring bad people to be good, or saying that they are not sinners after all. He is pronouncing them legally righteous, free from any liability to the broken law, because he himself in his Son has born the penalty of their law-breaking."[14] The payment of this penalty satisfies God's justice and thus provides the legal basis for our justification. As Paul will say a little later in Romans: "We have now been justified by his blood" (Rom. 5:9).

This saving truth brought lasting joy to William Cowper. Cowper is well known for his gospel hymns. What is perhaps less well known is that Cowper suffered a miserable childhood, which included the death of his mother and, afterwards, horrific bullying by some older boys. It is not surprising that throughout his life Cowper struggled with severe bouts of depression. Yet Cowper also knew the love of Jesus and his atoning work. Here is how he described his coming to Christ for justification:

> The happy period which was to shake off my fetters and afford me a clear opening of the free mercy of God in Christ Jesus was now arrived. I flung myself into a chair near the window, and, seeing a Bible there, ventured once more to apply to it for comfort and

instruction. The first verses I saw were in the third chapter of Romans: "Being justified freely by his grace through the redemption that is in Christ Jesus, whom God hath set forth to be a propitiation, through faith in his blood, to manifest his righteousness." Immediately I received strength to believe, and the full beams of the Sun of Righteousness shone on me. I saw the sufficiency of the atonement he had made, my pardon in his blood, and the fullness and completeness of his justification. In a moment I believed and received the gospel.[15]

"My pardon in his blood"—this phrase aptly summarizes the biblical doctrine of justification. Paul is explicit in calling us to put our faith in that pardoning blood, to believe in the atoning work of Christ on the cross. We are justified by faith, which is mentioned not less than six times in Romans 3: this righteousness from God comes "through *faith* in Jesus Christ for all who *believe*" (Rom. 3:22); God justifies "the one who has *faith* in Jesus" (Rom. 3:26); a person is "justified by *faith* apart from works of the law" (Rom. 3:28). The emphasis is unmistakable: we are justified by faith.

For our present purposes, what is said in verse 25 is especially noteworthy: we receive the blood of Jesus by faith. Today we are sometimes told that we need to get away from talking about the blood of Jesus. Yet the Bible presents the precious blood of Jesus as the atonement for our sins and thus as the object of justifying faith.

Atonement by Propitiation

Blood is mentioned again in connection with *propitiation*, which is a third term for atonement. God presented Jesus, or put him forward, "as a propitiation by his blood" (Rom. 3:25). Some translations prefer to speak here of "the sacrifice of atonement," but the proper word to use is *propitiation*.

Propitiation is a term for atonement that comes from the temple. To understand it, therefore, we need to go back to the atoning sacrifices that were made at the tabernacle in the wilderness, and later at the temple in Jerusalem.

The procedure for making atonement is perhaps most fully explained in Leviticus 16. The chapter begins with a warning intended to give the most serious impression of God's holiness. "The LORD said to Moses, 'Tell Aaron your brother not to come at any time into the Holy Place inside the veil, before the mercy seat that is on the ark, so that he may not die. For I will appear in the cloud over the mercy seat'" (Lev. 16:2).

This was not an idle threat but a necessary warning. The sons of Israel's first high priest had sauntered into the tabernacle and offered unholy fire, contrary to God's command. Immediately they perished (Lev. 10:1–2). God did this to show that he is too holy to be trifled with. Anyone who comes into his presence must come in the proper way, or else be consumed by fire.

Mercifully, God provided a way for sinners to approach him without being destroyed by his wrath. Once a year, Aaron was to make atonement for the sins of God's people. He would begin by offering a bull to atone for his own sins, as well as the sins of his household (Lev. 16:6, 11–14). Then he would take a perfect male goat and sacrifice it as a sin offering (Lev. 16:9). God said, "Then he shall kill the goat of the sin offering that is for the people and bring its blood inside the veil and do with its blood as he did with the blood of the bull, sprinkling it over the mercy seat and in front of the mercy seat" (Lev. 16:15). In this manner, the high priest "made atonement for himself and for his house and for all the assembly of Israel" (Lev. 16:17).

Symbolism in the Sacrifice

What did all this signify? The goat represented God's sinful people. In a symbolical way, the sins of God's people were transferred to the goat. Ordinarily, before an animal was sacrificed, the worshiper would place his hand on the animal's head while he confessed his sins (see Lev. 4:3). This was to show that the sinner's guilt was being charged or *imputed* to the animal. Then the animal was sacrificed on the altar. This was necessary because once the sins of the people were imputed to the goat, the goat had to suffer the deadly wages of sin. The goat was a substitute dying in the place of sinners, bearing their sins and then suffering the punishment that they deserved.

Once the sacrifice had been offered, the sacrificial blood functioned as the proof that atonement had been made for sin. This is made explicit in Leviticus 17:11, where God says, "It is the blood that makes atonement by the life." The reason that the blood takes away guilt is not because of its intrinsic properties, but because it shows that God has already carried out his death penalty against sin.

The symbolism of the blood is further clarified by its function in the Old Testament rituals of atonement. The high priest would take the blood and sprinkle it on the atonement cover, also called the mercy seat. The mercy seat was the golden lid on the Ark of the Covenant, located in the Most Holy Place of the temple, which was the earthly location of the Divine Presence. The mercy seat itself was a place of divine judgment, because the ark underneath the mercy seat contained the law of God, which the people had broken. Sprinkling blood on the mercy seat, therefore, was a way to put the blood of the atoning sacrifice between the holy God and his sinful people.

The sacrificial blood that was sprinkled on the mercy seat served as a propitiation for sin. This difficult word is necessary to use because it describes an essential truth of salvation. Propitiation refers to the turning away of anger. God's perfect justice has been satisfied, his righteous anger quenched. Propitiation thus explains what the atoning sacrifice accomplished with respect to God and his wrath.

God's Wrath

Here something needs to be said about the wrath of God, which is one of the most frequently mentioned divine attributes in the Bible. Wrath is not a violent emotion or uncontrollable passion but something more like righteous indignation. It is God's holy opposition to sin and his personal determination to punish it, what John Stott has defined as God's "steady, unrelenting, unremitting, uncompromising antagonism to evil in all its forms and manifestations."[16] Since it is right and good for God to hate every evil thing, wrath is one of his divine perfections. It is not something to be ashamed about, therefore, but something to be praised.

God's wrath against sin explains why the high priest never came into God's presence without the blood of an atoning sacrifice (Heb. 9:7). Remember Aaron's sons! If a priest came without the blood, he would be destroyed. Once the sacrifice had died in place of the sinner, however, no further punishment needed to be made. The priest sprinkled the blood on the mercy seat to show that God's justice was satisfied, his wrath propitiated. To say this another way, the sacrifice made God propitious, or well disposed, fully enabling him to look upon the sinner with favor.

Rather than accepting the biblical doctrine of propitiation, some theologians would prefer to deny God's wrath altogether. In fact, this is one of the main reasons why there are so many contemporary attacks on the doctrine of the atonement. Some theologians argue that what we really see at Calvary is not the wrath of God against human sin but only the wrath of humanity against God. According to one contemporary theologian, "In Jesus' own understanding of the Cross, the element of substitution appears when Jesus humbly endures the wrath of mankind instead of invoking the wrath of God upon us."[17]

This clever argument preserves the language of atonement and wrath yet never deals with the very real problem of the wrath of God. Praise God for Jesus Christ, who turns away the wrath of God by making full atonement for our sins! John Newton wrote about this atoning grace in his diary. Newton had been heavily involved in the slave trade and was guilty of many crimes against humanity and sins against God. As he lamented his lost and sinful condition he was weighed down with shame and tempted to despair. Yet when he was in the very depths, Newton looked to Christ and said, "But now I may, I must, I do mention the Atonement. I have sinned, but Christ has died."[18] Newton finally understood that atonement comes only through the death of Jesus Christ. His crucifixion is our substitution; his cross is our mercy seat; and the blood that Jesus sprinkled there is the propitiation of the wrath of God.

On rare but important occasions, the New Testament uses the language of propitiation to describe the saving work that Jesus did on the cross. We see this not only in Romans 3 but also in Hebrews 2, which describes Jesus as a "faithful high priest in the service of God, to make propitiation for the sins of the people" (Heb. 2:17). We see it as well in 1 John: "He is the propitiation for our sins" (1 John 2:2). Or again, "In this is love, not that we have loved God but that he loved us and sent his Son to be the propitiation for our sins" (1 John 4:10). Out of his great love for lost humanity, God has made atonement, quenching his own wrath in order that we might be saved.

The atonement is not a way of getting something that God does not want to give, therefore, but God's plan for reconciling sinners to himself. We should never think of propitiation as involving an angry Father reluctantly appeased by the death of his sweet Son. Christianity is far removed from such a pagan notion because the initiative for salvation always comes from the Father's loving heart. In the atonement and on the cross God propitiates God's own wrath. John Stott writes:

> It is God himself who in holy wrath needs to be propitiated, God himself who in holy love undertook to do the propitiating, and God himself who in the person of his Son died for the propitiation of our sins. Thus God took his own loving initiative to appease his own righteous anger by bearing it his own self in his own Son when he took our place and died for us. There is no crudity here to evoke our ridicule, only the profundity of holy love to evoke our worship.[19]

The Blood of the Atonement

As we consider the three terms for atonement that Paul offers in Romans 3—word pictures that come from the marketplace, the law court, and the temple—we should see that all three of them are associated with blood. Indeed, each of these aspects of atonement depends on the blood of Jesus for its efficacy. Atoning blood satisfies the deepest need of the human race.

In her book *Maya Mysteries*, Wendy Murray Zoba seeks to understand the need for atonement by examining the bloodiness of the ancient Mayan system of sacrifice. History and archaeology show that the Maya practiced elaborate rituals of atonement, centered on child sacrifice. As Zoba explains,

> The Maya understood the need for blood, especially the blood. They have shown us there isn't enough human blood in all the world to satisfy the gods. They are telling us the power of the sacrifice cannot be found in the blood of humans sacrificed by human hands. When the warfare increased toward the end of the dynasty, and the Maya all over the lowlands fought their civil wars and took captives, did they send them to the fields to work? No. They cut off their heads and carried them on sticks. For what? What did all that blood avail the ancient Maya?[20]

The answer is that blood availed them nothing. The Maya thought that offering human sacrifices would bring them closer to God. But the gods were not appeased, even when the bloodletting intensified. As Zoba concludes, "The gods were not satisfied," and thus the Maya did not receive forgiveness for their sins.

To us the ancient Mayan rituals seem primitive and barbaric. Yet many people feel the same way about the sacrifices of the Old Testament, and even about the crucifixion of Jesus Christ. What do bloody sacrifices have to do with daily life in a postmodern world? One late-night comedian mocked Christianity by saying, "You can't be a rational person six days of the week . . . and on one day of the week go to a building and think you are drinking the blood of a 2,000-year-old space God. . . . That makes you a schizophrenic."[21]

Believing in the blood of God is not schizophrenic; it is the gospel that holds everything together. The need for atoning blood is a universal principle of divine justice for all peoples, in all places, at all times. The human race has fallen into sin. We have turned against God in rebellion, refusing to obey him, and choosing instead to go our own way. As a result, we deserve to die. This is what God's justice demands. We have sinned against his infinite majesty, and nothing less than life itself can pay the debt that we owe. Blood is the price for sin, the only thing that can make us right with God. Though the Maya were wrong about many things, they were right about this (much "righter" than many people today): deep down, they knew that blood is the way to God.

We see blood in every aspect of the atonement. The blood of Jesus is our redemption—the payment of the price for our freedom from sin. His blood is our justification—the legal basis for the declaration of our righteousness before God. His blood is our propitiation—our protection from the wrath of God. The wonder of the atonement is that we are saved by the shedding of blood, not our own blood but the blood that God has shed for our sins.

Believing the Doctrine

The primary thing for us to do with this great doctrine of the atonement is to believe it. Believe that Jesus has paid the ransom price for your redemption. Believe that you are declared righteous before God in your justification. Believe that the blood of Jesus is the propitiation for your sins. Believe in Jesus Christ and his atoning work on the cross.

Then worship what you believe, praising Jesus for the gift of his atoning blood. It is characteristic of any healthy community of Christian faith that it is explicit in praising God for the precious blood of Jesus Christ. Thus the blood of Jesus is a recurring theme in many great hymns of the Christian faith, including this one by William Cowper:

There is a fountain filled with blood,
Drawn from Immanuel's veins;
And sinners, plunged beneath that flood,
Lose all their guilty stains.

The dying thief rejoiced to see
That fountain in his day
And there have I, as vile as he,
Washed all my sins away.

In addition to believing and worshiping, there is something more for us to do in response to Jesus and his atoning blood. We ourselves are now called to a life of costly sacrifice. What sacrifice could ever be too great for us to offer to the Savior, who has shed his own blood for our sins?

We are called, therefore, to sacrifice in every aspect of our Christian experience. We are called to sacrifice in the stewardship of our financial resources. Whenever we are giving to kingdom work, or praying about what to give, we should remember the blood that Jesus paid for our sins.

We are called to sacrifice in our homes and neighborhoods, setting aside our own agendas to spend more time with friends who need to know the love of Jesus. We are called to sacrifice for our families, putting others first in the life of the home. We are called to sacrifice in marriage, especially those of us who are husbands, and who are therefore called to show the sacrifice of the cross in loving our wives (see Eph. 5:25–33).

We are also called to sacrifice in ministry. I witnessed this firsthand in the life of the late Reverend William Still, who for more than fifty years served Gilcomston South Presbyterian Church in downtown Aberdeen. When the Scottish minister wrote his spiritual autobiography, he gave it a title that encapsulated his philosophy of ministry: *Dying to Live*. Mr. Still wrote:

> From the moment that you stand there dead in Christ and dead to everything you are and have and ever shall be and have, every breath you breathe thereafter, every thought you think, every word you say and deed you do, must be done over the top of your own corpse or reaching over it in your preaching to others. Then it can only be Jesus that comes over and no one else. And I believe that every preacher must bear the mark of that death. Your life must be signed by the Cross, not just Christ's Cross (there is really no other) but your cross in his Cross, your particular and unique cross that no one ever died—the cross that no one ever could die but you and you alone: your death in Christ's death.[22]

This principle is not just for ministers but for every believer in Jesus Christ. All of us are called to bear the mark of the blood atonement of Jesus Christ. The precious blood of Jesus Christ calls us to sacrifice in every aspect of our Christian experience. This is what a Christian is: someone who says to Jesus, in word and deed, "You have shed your blood for me; now I give my life to you."

CLEANSING BLOOD

Richard D. Phillips

For if the blood of goats and bulls, and the sprinkling of defiled persons with the ashes of a heifer, sanctify for the purification of the flesh, how much more will the blood of Christ, who through the eternal Spirit offered himself without blemish to God, purify our conscience from dead works to serve the living God.

—Hebrews 9:13–14

Charles Colson tells of watching a television interview with Albert Speer, Adolf Hitler's confidant and industrialist, who, after World War II, was stricken with a great sense of guilt for the horrors he had assisted. Speer was one of the few war criminals tried at Nuremburg to admit his guilt, for which he served twenty years in Spandau prison. In one of his books he commented that his guilt never could nor should be forgiven and that he would forever be seeking to atone for his sins. Commenting on this, his interviewer pressed him as to whether it would ever be possible for him to be forgiven. Speer shook his head, replying, "I don't think it will be possible." Colson remarks on Speer's obvious desperation. "I wanted to write Speer," he recalls, "to tell him about Jesus and his death on the cross, about God's forgiveness. But there wasn't time. [That] interview was his last public statement; he died shortly after."[1]

What Speer needed, and the Christian gospel provides, is cleansing from his sin through the blood of Christ. We have been considering Christ's atoning work, so far focusing on the atonement as redemption and propitiation. We are bought back from sin by Christ's redeeming blood, and God's just wrath toward us is turned aside by Christ's substitutionary suffering. In other words, we have considered the atonement as it relates to sin and as it relates to God. But what about ourselves? Can we ever be cleansed so that our hearts are free from the stain of sin? Speer answered *no*, not knowing the cross of Christ. Colson, knowing the grace of Jesus, pointed to the cross and answered with a glorious *yes*.

Indeed, the cleansing of our sin by the precious blood of Christ is something to sing about. And how God's people have sung to this wonderful theme! We sing:

> *Wash me, make me pure within, Cleanse, O cleanse me from my sin.*[2]

> *Foul, I, to the fountain fly / Wash me, Savior, or I die.*[3]

> *There is a fountain filled with blood, drawn from Immanuel's veins;*
> *And sinners, plunged beneath that flood, lose all their guilty stains.*[4]

Expiation: A Neglected Theme

Given the priority in popular Christian piety of the cleansing of our sins, it is surprising that doctrinal treatments of the atonement often neglect this theme. A typical example is John Stott's outstanding book *The Cross of Christ*. In his chapter on the cross and salvation, Stott thoroughly details the atonement as propitiation, as redemption, as justification, and as reconciliation.[5] But virtually no consideration is given to expiation, the actual removal or cleansing of our sins, as so clearly stated by our text. On the one occasion when Hebrews 9:14

is referenced, it is cited only to amplify the point of Christ as our substitute, since the verse states that he "offered himself."[6]

The apparent reason for this neglect of the cleansing effects of Christ's blood on the conscience is the polemic context in which Stott was writing. For a generation and more, expiation had taken the place of propitiation in scholarly consideration of the atonement, the latter of which was vigorously denied.

Following Leon Morris's overwhelming defense of propitiation in *The Apostolic Preaching of the Cross*,[7] the generation of evangelicals prior to ours was determined to reestablish propitiation. That is, Stott and others[8] wished to show that the cross not only has effects on the sinner but that Christ's death changes God's stance towards us from wrath to acceptance. But as a result, little attention was given to the reality that Christ's blood does cleanse the sinner. This neglect of expiation is found in numerous treatments of the atonement, with the result that one of the blessings of the cross that is closest to our hearts is left absent from many minds.

Expiation in Scripture

The theme of expiation was not absent from the mind of the writer of Hebrews. His is the New Testament book that most clearly describes the cleansing of our sins through Christ's blood. It was only natural, after all, for the writer of Hebrews to present Christ's atonement in terms of the fulfillment of the Old Testament priesthood, which focused so strongly on the removal of sin. For when Jewish believers thought about Jesus as the sacrificial Lamb of God, they thought not only of a hill far away and an old rugged cross, but they thought also of the temple. It was at the temple that the blood of the lamb opened the way into the presence of God. Thus it was a distinctively Jewish—that is, Old Testament—message that Hebrews 9:14 gives in stating that the blood of Christ will "purify our conscience from dead works to serve the living God."

In many respects, Hebrews is an extended commentary on the book of Leviticus, which details the ceremonial law and the temple ritual of the Jews. Leviticus 12 to 15 details the ceremonies for cleansing from defilement. Those who ate forbidden meats were rendered unfit for the presence of God. People with skin diseases such as leprosy were unclean. Women with an issue of blood were ceremonially unclean, since blood was a sign of death. These situations were pictures of sin and its effects and were a way of showing that only the spotless and pure could come into God's presence. The work of the priests, then, was to make sure that everyone who entered the temple was clean.

If a person had a skin rash or a spot on his skin, the priest was to inspect it. If it was infectious, the priest would pronounce the person unclean. Such a person was barred from entering the temple precincts and was quarantined, and he or she remained unclean as long as the situation persisted. The plight of lepers was especially sorrowful. God told Moses, "Command the people of Israel that they put out of the camp everyone who is leprous or has a discharge and everyone who is unclean through contact with the dead" (Num. 5:1–2). Leviticus directs such people to "cry out, 'Unclean, unclean'" when anyone drew near to be sure that no contact was made and no one else was contaminated (Lev. 13:45). "He shall remain unclean as long as he has the disease. He is unclean. He shall live alone. His dwelling shall be outside the camp" (Lev. 13:46).

In her excellent commentary on Leviticus, designed to make the book plain to children, Nancy Ganz explains the purposes for these procedures. First, the unclean were quarantined for the physical well-being of Israel. "Physically, it was a very real protection for God's people that carriers of contagious diseases were isolated outside the camp, separated from the rest of the community, to keep the infectious diseases from spreading." Second, the status of the unclean made an essential spiritual point: "Spiritually, it was a very real proclamation to God's people that the Lord was a holy

God and that they must be a holy people. Sin must be eradicated from their lives."[9]

Through this and other ways, God was impressing upon his people the seriousness of sin and the dread reality of their spiritual condition. Ganz writes: "If this was how seriously a surface corruption (such as a skin disease) could separate a person from God and the community of the saints, imagine how wide was the chasm caused by the deep inner corruption of the heart and soul by unrestrained and unremoved sin."[10] The prophet Isaiah made this very application in his preaching on the sinful condition of the people: "We have all become like one who is unclean, and all our righteous deeds are like a polluted garment" (Isa. 64:6).

The good news was that if the unclean situation was removed, there were rituals for his reinstatement to society and the temple. The procedure for this was particularly vivid. After an inspection in which the priest verified that the disease was healed, the priest was to take two live birds, along with cedarwood, scarlet yarn, and hyssop (Lev. 14:1–4). One bird was to be killed in a pot filled with fresh water. The live bird would have the red cedarwood tied to it with the scarlet yarn and was then dipped seven times in the water stained with the dead bird's blood. The same bloody water was to be sprinkled on the former leper. Then the leper would be declared clean and the live bird let go to fly away.

Here are the two great halves of the atoning work of Christ: expiation and propitiation. Just as the leper was declared ceremonially clean, so also Christ removes the stain of sin from us. The live bird, sprinkled with blood and colored red by the cedarwood and scarlet yarn, depicted our complete forgiveness from sin. How? By propitiation; that is, by the death of the first bird as a substitute for our sins. As our minds see that red-stained bird ascend farther and farther out of sight, we remember the words of Psalm 103:12, "As far as the east is from the west, so far does he remove our transgressions from us."

Perfected by Sacrifice

This is precisely the writer of Hebrews' concern in 9:14: "How much more will the blood of Christ, who through the eternal Spirit offered himself without blemish to God, purify our conscience from dead works to serve the living God." His concern is the effect of sin in barring us from God's presence and service. His favorite word for the atonement's remedy is *perfected*. We see it in Hebrews 10:14, where he makes a similar point: "For by a single offering he has perfected for all time those who are being sanctified."

The language of "perfecting" has the connotation of "consecrating"; priests in the temple perfected or consecrated themselves for service before God by cleansing their bodies and donning priestly clothes. In Hebrews 9:11–13, the writer makes two points with this respect. In verse 13, he points out that "if the blood of goats and bulls, and the sprinkling of defiled persons with the ashes of a heifer"—mentioning still more rites prescribed by Leviticus, but referring to them all—sanctifies "for the purification of the flesh." His point was that the rituals given to the Levitical priests enabled them to restore people with leprosy and other defilements to the holy precincts of God. They were successful in removing ritual defilement. But he points out that Christ, by his priestly ministry, has done so much more:

> But when Christ appeared as a high priest of the good things that have come, then through the greater and more perfect tent (not made with hands, that is, not of this creation) he entered once for all into the holy places, not by means of the blood of goats and calves but by means of his own blood, thus securing an eternal redemption. (Heb. 9:11–12)

You see his point: here is the real thing! The old covenant rituals were symbolic of expiation, even as the ritual defilements were symbolic of sin. A leper would be cleansed by means of the two birds, and the tabernacle would be sanctified by the application of the ashes of a red heifer (cf. Num. 19:1–10). But it was symbolism. It was only flesh. In contrast, what Christ has done is real. His blood cleanses not merely the symbols of sin but sin itself.

Notice that the basis of our cleansing, our expiation, is propitiation, along with redemption. Christ ascended into the heavenly temple of the presence of God the Father and presented the finished work of the atonement. The writer of Hebrews expresses this in tabernacle/temple language: Jesus entered "the greater and more perfect tent (not made with hands, that is, not of this creation" (Heb. 9:11). He entered the heavenly temple of God. There, Jesus presented for us not merely animal blood symbolically spilled—the purpose of which had always been merely to show the need for a more perfect sacrifice—but Jesus presented "his own blood" (Heb. 9:12). The precious blood of God the Son redeems us from our debt to God's perfect justice, possessing more than enough value to pay the debt of our sin.

Moreover, having poured out the infinite wrath that our sins deserve upon Jesus, the holy God is propitiated. His justice is satisfied and his wrath turned away. The result is the cleansing of our sins before God, so that like the leper who was healed and his body ritually cleansed, we are newly consecrated with the true sacrificial blood, and our sins are washed away.

Consecrated Worship

Let me apply this in two settings. The first is the worship of God's people in the church. I am firmly convinced that a redemptively configured worship service ought to include a confession of sin and pronouncement of gospel pardon to the congregation. One reason for this is the great danger that we might think ourselves worthy on our own to come into God's presence. Isn't it a danger for religious people like us to think, "How happy God must be to have people like us to worship him! Of course he accepts us, since we are religious, believing people!"

But just as Cain was rebuffed when he approached God at the gate of the garden with the produce of his fields—which was a picture of his good works—we need to face the reality that our good works do not gain us entry into the presence of the holy God. The simple reason is that Isaiah was right: we are like the unclean, and even our supposedly righteous works are polluted with sin (Isa. 64:6). The only way for sinners like us to come into God's holy presence is by way of the atoning blood of Christ. Therefore, we should come confessing our sins and looking to the cross for our entry into worship.

But there is a corollary to this that is equally important. For not only *may we not* come *apart* from Christ's blood, we *may* indeed come to God *through* the precious blood of Christ. How many of us, subconsciously or consciously, come to worship expecting to be kept outside by God? We are burdened by our failures. We feel unworthy and ashamed. All of this keeps us from drawing our hearts near to God. What's the point? God either won't or can't really receive people like us with open arms. We think, *how could a holy God accept a sinner like me?* The answer is the cleansing blood of Christ.

When Christ has paid our penalty and redeemed us by his blood, our sins are removed from God's presence. They are paid and punished. This was one of the great promises of the new covenant in Christ, so carefully recited from Jeremiah by the writer of Hebrews. Not only does God say, "I will be merciful toward their iniquities," but he adds, "I will remember their sins no more" (Heb. 8:12). So far as God is concerned, our sins are not there anymore. They have been removed. We have been cleansed by the blood of Jesus.

Personal Piety

The same situation pertains to our personal piety, especially to prayer. Again, we need to realize that God has not promised to answer the prayers of those whose sins are not forgiven. It is only "in Christ's name" that we may confidently pray. But how many of us remain spiritually aloof from God, reluctant and hesitant to pray, because we think that God must surely have it out for us? But Paul responds, "Through [Christ] we both have access . . . to the Father" (Eph. 2:18).

Let me put it this way: through the blood of Christ, from which you benefit by simple faith, everything that rightly stands between you and God has been removed by the cross. The sins that must surely make God look on you with loathing—and they would!—have been washed clean by the precious blood of Jesus. Our reality in Christ is that depicted by Isaiah: "As the bridegroom rejoices over the bride, so shall your God rejoice over you" (Isa. 62:5).

I have had the privilege of presiding at a good many weddings. And I can assure you that when the back doors open and the bride appears in all her gleaming beauty, the groom's face is filled with rapturous love and delight. Cleansed white as snow by the blood of Christ and clothed by the imputation of his gloriously perfect righteousness, we stand before God every day of our lives as a bride stands before her groom on the wedding day.

How important it is for us to know this! We are cleansed by the blood of Christ. We are washed clean as snow. So let us come to him, our loving God, and to Christ, our delighted groom. Let us approach worship with the thrill of acceptance into God's blessing, and let us lift up our hearts in prayer with thanksgiving for God's tender mercies in Christ.

A Better Priest

The particular burden of the writer of Hebrews was to prove to his Jewish Christian audience that Jesus is a better priest than those of the old covenant. He wanted them to stand fast in the face of persecution, refusing to let go of the one and only Savior. They were being barred from the temple services and the communal life of Israel because of their insistence that Jesus is the Messiah. That was a loss, but nothing compared to the loss of salvation in Christ.

Consider the Levitical priests again. They had the authority to declare clean those who had been made clean. But they lacked the

power to *make* sinners clean. They could declare someone healed
of leprosy to be eligible to rejoin worship. But they could not heal.
How much more does the blood of Christ do for us! John puts it in
clear terms: "The blood of Jesus [God's] Son cleanses us from all sin"
(1 John 1:7). Jesus does not merely declare pure those who have been
made pure. He makes us pure through his cleansing blood.

When we consider the Gospel accounts of Jesus healing lepers,
we see why it is his blood we trust alone, not either the consecration
of Jewish priests or the absolution of ministers today. Luke tells us
that as Jesus was going by, a leper spied him. How wretched the
leper was in the corruption of his body and in the miserable isolation
of his uncleanness! So he fell before Jesus, begging him, "Lord, if
you will, you can make me clean" (Luke 5:12). This shows us that
the first step in our cleansing is to believe that the precious blood
of Jesus, God's divine Son, is able to cleanse us from sin. And how
willing Jesus was: "I will," he replied; "be clean" (v. 13).

Luke says that the man was "full of leprosy," and in a lovely
parallel, Mark's version of this episode tells us that Jesus was "filled
with compassion" (Mark 1:41 NIV). This is why we need cleansing,
for as the poor man was filled with leprosy, we are filled with uncleanness, filled with impurity. But Jesus meets our need. Not only
can he cleanse us, but he is filled with mercy for us.

Jesus came into this world to know us in our sufferings, to feel the
pang of thirst and the weariness of the flesh. He came and suffered
temptation himself, and therefore he is able, even as God, to sympa-
thize with our suffering and our trials. Jesus is willing to cleanse you,
not because of what is in you, not because you are lovely or lovable,
but because of what is in him. He is "filled with compassion." And
that is why he is willing.

Notice, too, a detail Luke provides. Before Jesus cleansed the man,
Luke tells us he "stretched out his hand and touched him" (Luke
5:13). I think the touch of Jesus' hand was completely astonishing
to this leper. He believed that Jesus could make him clean, but surely

he did not dream that Jesus would touch him. He dared to hope this healer would cure him, but he dared not hope he would place his warm, human hands upon his wretched skin. But Jesus did not first cleanse the leper and then touch him; he touched him in his unclean state. And then, only then, did he declare with power, "Be clean."

What does this say about Jesus' attitude toward you, in the reality of your impure heart, your unclean body and spirit? Surely this means that he is willing to reach into whatever garbage heap you are to be found, willing to reach through the sewage that clings to your soul, willing to touch you as you are, in order to have fellowship with you, as Savior and Lord, and to cleanse you from your sin.

A Cleansed Conscience

But there is one last matter of cleansing before we can be truly restored to God's presence. When Jesus died for our sins on the cross and then presented himself in the presence of God as our redeemer, he cleansed our sins before the Father. But there is a cleansing inside of us that also needs to take place.

We don't often think about our conscience as a serious problem, a barrier, when it comes to our relationship with God. After all, the problem is what God thinks about us, not what we think about ourselves. But even after God has accepted us in Christ, our unclean conscience can keep us far from God. Christ's ministry as high priest is to actually bring us to God. Therefore, he not only reconciles God to us, but he also cleanses our consciences so that we may be willing to enter into his service.

The conscience serves to tell us about ourselves. It communicates to us what we are. Charles Spurgeon, in his sermon on this text, pointed out three problems revealed by our conscience: a knowledge of past sinful acts; a knowledge of our sinful nature, with its thoughts and desires; and our ongoing contact with sin in this world. All of these conspire, unless cleansed, to keep us from serving the Lord. About the first of these, Spurgeon writes:

Upon our consciences there rests, first of all, a sense of past sin. Even if a man wishes to serve God, yet until his conscience is purged, he feels a dread and terror of God which prevent his doing so. He has sinned, and God is just, and therefore he is ill at ease. . . . "God is angry with the wicked every day, if he turn not he will whet his sword; he hath bent his bow, and made it ready"; and the sinner, knowing this, asks, "How can I serve this terrible God?" He is alarmed when he thinks of the judge of all the earth; for it is before that Judge that he will soon have to take his trial.[11]

Christ's blood, however, possesses power to cleanse this great fear from our hearts, this condemnation from our consciences. His death preaches to us that the debt has been paid for all of our sin; an infinite atonement has been made for us, to relieve us of the burden of so great a guilt. This is what causes Christians to sing about the shedding of Christ's innocent blood, for in it we see our guilt washed away.

There is no greater burden than the guilt of sins we have committed. Other burdens weary the feet or the back; this burden wearies the soul. People may try to ignore this fact. People may write platitudes about the goodness of man. People may say that we are merely finding our destiny out of a Darwinian soup, perhaps not yet what we might be, not really whole, but certainly not guilty. But for the real man and woman in this world, such words will not wash. They will not wash away the knowledge of things we have done in a universe with moral reality over which stands a real and holy God.

How, then, can robes be washed in blood and come out white? The answer is that Christ's shed blood on the cross, "who through the eternal Spirit offered himself without blemish to God" (Heb. 9:14), is the cleansing agent provided by God for the only truly lasting stain, the stain of the guilt of our sin. Christ's sacrifice was not merely physical but also spiritual, and through the ministry of the Holy Spirit he preaches forgiveness of sin to our hearts: "Though your sins are like scarlet," his blood says, "they shall be as white as snow" (Isa. 1:18).

What about the second burden on the conscience, the awareness of present sinful desires and thoughts, the knowledge not merely of our sinful deeds but of our sinful nature? This, too, is cleansed by the blood of the Lamb. We feel unclean, and this keeps us from God. We are like Isaiah, with access to see the seraphim praising God in his temple, crying, "Holy, holy, holy is the LORD of hosts." At such a sight we cry, "Woe is me! For I am lost; for I am a man of unclean lips." Don't we experience that when we draw near to God? But Jesus, like the angel in Isaiah's vision, flies to grasp a coal from the altar on which his own blood was shed and presses it to our lips. "Behold,' he says, "your guilt is taken away, and your sin is atoned for" (Isa. 6:3–7).

Our conscience tells us what we must think of ourselves; but the blood of Christ tells us what God thinks of us. And since Jesus offered a spiritual sacrifice on the cross—not suffering merely in body but rending his spirit for our cleansing—the Holy Spirit he sends cleanses us in spirit. Jesus stands there with basin and towel in hand and says, "You are clean" (John 13:10).

Finally, our conscience recoils as we walk through this world, brushing against and being drawn into sin of all kinds, bringing defilement just as contact with death did to the Israelites of old. But as Israel's priests sprinkled the blood of bulls and goats upon the skin, we have in Christ a ready cleansing for daily sins. "If we confess our sins," 1 John 1:9 tells us, "he is faithful and just to forgive us our sins and to cleanse us from all unrighteousness." We have cleansing through the blood of Jesus. As Isaac Watts writes in a hymn:

> *Not all the blood of beasts on Jewish altars slain,*
> *Could give the guilty conscience peace, or wash away the stain;*
> *But Christ, the heavenly Lamb, takes all our sins away,*
> *A sacrifice of nobler name and richer blood than they.*

Confidence before God

The writer of Hebrews wanted his readers to hold fast to Jesus despite all persecution. For how can we be saved if we let go of Jesus? As he puts it, "How shall we escape if we neglect such a great salvation?" (Heb. 2:3). Therefore, he preaches, don't let anything cause you to turn away from Jesus. He is our only Redeemer, and his is the only blood that cleanses us from sin.

Every pastor knows the need of Christians for such encouragement. How many walk in danger because of discouragement or because of temptation to fall away when under trials? But there is also a positive exhortation, and with this the writer of Hebrews brings the doctrinal section of his letter to an end. It is a plea to enter fully into the life in Christ:

> Therefore, brothers, since we have confidence to enter the holy places by the blood of Jesus, by the new and living way that he opened for us through the curtain, that is, through his flesh, and since we have a great priest over the house of God, let us draw near with a true heart in full assurance of faith, with our hearts sprinkled clean from an evil conscience and our bodies washed with pure water. Let us hold fast the confession of our hope without wavering, for he who promised is faithful. And let us consider how to stir up one another to love and good works, not neglecting to meet together, as is the habit of some, but encouraging one another, and all the more as you see the Day drawing near. (Heb. 10:19–25)

Do you get his point? Let us live like the cleansed people that we are. Let us have confidence in our relationship with God, not because of some worthiness in ourselves but because of the preciousness of that atoning blood shed for us. What a tragedy it would be for Christian people—those who are truly cleansed by Christ's blood—to spend our days dreading God! Instead, let us draw near to our Father, having the assurance of our faith that our souls are washed clean, our hearts consecrated by Jesus for fellowship with God through the sprinkling of his blood.

When all else seems to fail, let us hold onto these words: "The blood of Jesus [God's] Son cleanses us from all sin" (1 John 1:7). And then let us live for God with passion and purpose, devoting ourselves to the good work of his kingdom, caring for one another in Christian love, always casting our eye to the horizon, where Jesus will soon return in glory, thus able to face death and, more importantly, to face life with joy and peace.

I began this chapter by mentioning Albert Speer, the Nazi war criminal who believed that nothing could ever forgive his horrific sins against so many. I want to close with the testimony of several other Nazi war criminals. Their story involves Henry Gerecke, the Lutheran minister assigned as chaplain to that remarkable collection of inmates. Gerecke looked on this band of Hitler's closest associates with the love of Christ. He met with them one-on-one, seeking to learn the state of their hearts as they faced public humiliation and likely execution. He began a chapel service, and many of the Nazi hierarchy attended.

After a few weeks under Gerecke's simple gospel preaching, eight of them professed faith in Jesus Christ and were admitted to the Lord's Table. Among them were field marshal Wilhelm Keitel, chief of the German Armed Forces; Fritz Sauckel, Nazi head of labor supply, described as the cruelest slave master since Pharaoh; and Wilhelm Frick, the minister of the interior, who oversaw a reign of terror that had targeted many Christians. Also included was Joachim von Ribbentrop, Germany's foreign minister, who labored beside Hitler to deceive other nations and plunge the world into war. When Ribbentrop first met with Gerecke, he responded with a litany of scornful, intellectual objections to the Christian faith. But he attended the chapel services, and under the faithful gospel preaching, God's Word was pressed to his heart, and he was thoroughly converted.

Finally, the long-awaited end came to the Nuremburg Christians, in the early hours of October 16, 1946. Ribbentrop was summoned first, and it was Pastor Gerecke who came for him. Together they walked down the corridor and then onto the scaffold. As the noose was placed over the former foreign minister's head, he was asked for his last words. Anticipating this moment, he had perhaps planned to maintain loyalty to his Führer, departing life with a loud "Heil, Hitler!" But instead, he expressed his allegiance and faith to his new Master, discovered in the pages of the Bible. He calmly spoke: "I place all my confidence in the Lamb who made atonement for my sins. May God have mercy on my soul."[12] As the writer of Hebrews advised, the new-born Christian Ribbentrop had "confidence to enter the holy places by the blood of Jesus," his heart "sprinkled clean from an evil conscience" and his soul washed clean before God.

Can a Nazi war criminal find forgiveness and a cleansed conscience through the blood of Christ? Of course he can, for the blood of God's Son is precious beyond measure, fully able to pay the greatest debt of sin and, by the power of his Spirit, fully able to cleanse the conscience. It is with this faith that each of us is enabled to face death and the waiting judgment of God: "I place all my confidence in the Lamb who made atonement for my sins." And it is that faith with which we can face life, with hope and peace, joyfully living now to serve and worship him. "The blood of Jesus [God's] Son cleanses us from all sin" (1 John 1:7).

OFFENSIVE BLOOD

W. Robert Godfrey

For his sake I have suffered the loss of all things and count them as rubbish, in order that I may gain Christ and be found in him, not having a righteousness of my own that comes from the law, but that which comes through faith in Christ, the righteousness from God that depends on faith.

—Philippians 3:8–9

Jesus once declared, "Blessed is the one who is not offended by me" (Matt. 11:6; Luke 7:23). Whenever I see those words, I want to ask, "How could someone be offended by Jesus? Is not Jesus the Lord of love? Is not Jesus the Lord of life?" Jesus never once in his life did one sinful thing. He is the one upon whom we meditate as altogether good, altogether lovely, and altogether beautiful. It doesn't matter how carefully we study the scriptural accounts of him or how deeply we meditate upon his character, both now in this life and so much more profoundly in the life of the world to come; no matter how much we get to know Jesus, all we will find there is goodness and love. So how can it be that Jesus can say, "Blessed is the one who is not offended by me"?

Forms of Offense

Yet we know that many in this world are offended by him, and that offense takes a number of different forms. Sometimes it seems relatively benign. Some say, "Oh, no, I know Jesus. I love Jesus. I follow Jesus. Let me explain Jesus to you." But we discover that the Jesus they claim to know and love is not at all the Jesus of the Scriptures.

I have a growing sense of alarm as I walk into secular bookstores and find an ever-growing religious section there. How many of those books about Jesus are entirely unreliable? An example I recently saw is a book by Deepak Chopra, who, as a New Age guru, is not a reliable guide to truth. His new book is entitled *The Third Jesus*. I didn't even look at the table of contents, since I found the title so alarming. (I fear he probably got the first Jesus and the second Jesus wrong, too.) But there are many like him who take the name of Jesus on their lips yet reduce him to a mere teacher or moral example that we should follow. In doing so they reveal, of course, that they are offended by the Jesus of the Bible. They have not really listened to the word of our Savior when he says, "Blessed is the one who is not offended by me."

Strikingly, these words were addressed to none other than John the Baptist. John had sent messengers to inquire, "Are you the one who is to come, or shall we look for another?" (Matt. 11:3). John was probably not in doubt that Jesus was the Savior, but he may have been a bit impatient with the way Jesus was going about his messianic work, possibly somewhat infected by the expectation that when the Messiah first came to earth, he would come in glory, that he would vindicate his people speedily and establish the promised eternal kingdom.

John sends this inquiry when he is in prison, disappointed in the Messiah. We can imagine him thinking, "Why am I in prison? Why am I suffering? If you are the one, why aren't you going about your work more quickly to make all things new?" Jesus in response told John's disciples to report to John what they were seeing and hearing: the blind were being given sight, the lame were made able to walk, lepers were being cleansed, the deaf could hear, the dead were being raised, and good news was being preached to the poor (Matt. 11:4–5).

If Jesus had been more rapid in setting up the glory of his kingdom, you and I would have been left out. But Jesus was concerned about all who would need to hear about his love and would need to experience his forgiveness. So he took the cross upon himself and calls us as his people to follow in taking ourselves upon the path of suffering, humiliation, and lowliness so that the gospel might continue to be preached and the elect from every part of the world might be gathered. Jesus is saying to John and to you and me, "I know what I'm doing. My timetable may not be your timetable, but I know what I'm doing. In fact I'm Messiah. Trust me." "Blessed is the one who is not offended by me" (Matt. 11:6).

There are some, then, who are offended by Jesus in a rather benign way; though, of course, taking offense at Jesus is never genuinely benign. There are also those who take a much more virulent opposition to Jesus. Paul, in Philippians 3:18, reminds us of this sad fact: "For many, of whom I have often told you and now tell you even with tears, walk as enemies of the cross of Christ." Jesus has enemies, and those enemies take particular offense at him and at his cross, which should not surprise us if we know the Scriptures.

This particularly should not surprise us if we know the book of Psalms. It will be striking to anyone who studies the psalms that opposition to God seems to be a constant theme. This theme may even be somewhat troubling. But the psalms remind us that great works have great enemies, and that this world sadly abounds with enemies of the cross—enemies who oppose Christ without a cause.

David writes as a prophet about his own experience, but he writes even more truly about the experience of Jesus Christ. Consider, for instance, Psalm 69:4: "More in number than the hairs of my head are those who hate me without cause; mighty are those who would destroy me, those who attack me with lies. What I did not steal must I now restore?" Jesus was hated without a cause. That is what we, as Christians, sense deep in our souls when we see opposition to Jesus Christ. Why should he be hated, why should he be rejected, when he is good, loving, and kind? Yet the truth is that he is rejected.

Another remarkable psalm of David, Psalm 109, also leads us into the mind of Jesus. It is not difficult to imagine that the Savior might have prayed this psalm in Gethsemane. We read in verses 4 and 5, "In return for my love they accuse me, but I give myself to prayer. So they reward me evil for good, and hatred for my love." Is this not a picture of the Savior? He went around only doing good and loving, and he was hated by many. He was returned evil for the good that he did to many. He was accused, though all he had done was to love.

That is the sad kind of world in which we live, the world with which we have to cope as we think about the offense of the blood of Jesus Christ. Christ's blood is offensive to this world on a number of levels. Perhaps the best summary is to observe that the world is offended by the Christ of the cross and the cross of the Christ.

Offended by the Christ of the Cross

The world is, first of all, offended by the Christ of the cross. The world is offended by Christ as he really is, as he revealed himself in his coming, and as the Scriptures testify of him. This is the Christ Paul speaks of seeking to know in Philippians 3:7: "Whatever gain I had, I counted as loss for the sake of Christ." It is as if Paul is saying, "Nothing I have counts for anything in knowing Christ. I want Christ to be all to me. I want Christ to be the center and the foundation and the heart and the soul of my life. I want to be able to say that, for me, to live is Christ and to die is gain because I'll know Christ better in the glory that is to come.

Paul's focus is on Christ because Christ is exalted above all things. Paul has earlier celebrated Christ in Philippians 2: Christ is the eternal

Word, filled with the glory of the Godhead, sharing equally as the Son with the Father and the Spirit in divinity, glory, and eternality. This glorious Son is the one who is made flesh and is now again exalted by the Father and seated at his right hand. We are promised that as God has exalted him, so God will one day give him visible triumph (Phil. 2:1–11). In Philippians 2:9–11 we read similar words of adoring praise: "Therefore God has highly exalted him and bestowed on him the name that is above every name, so that at the name of Jesus every knee should bow, in heaven and on earth and under the earth, and every tongue confess that Jesus Christ is Lord, to the glory of God the Father."

What a wonderful declaration, Jesus is Lord! Jesus is the name above every name. One day, at the name of Jesus, every knee will bow, and every tongue confess that he is Lord. We, as Christians, find our souls stirred by that declaration of the apostle. Our faith is stimulated, and we look forward to that great day with longing; even so, come Lord Jesus.

But there seems to be a growing chorus of voices in our world that says, "This is exactly the source of problem and difficulty and violence in our world! The claim that Jesus is the name above every other name causes trouble in this world because it sets Christian against Jew, Christian against Muslim, Christian against Hindu, and Christian against atheist." We are told: "Don't you know that most of the problems in the world are a result of this kind of exclusivism, this kind of triumphalism? Most of the problems in this world are really the result of the kind of monotheism that we find expressed here—a monotheism that is so bigoted in its claim to knowing the only truth."

Have you heard this complaint against Christianity? Have you heard this kind of complaint against you? Some fear that this criticism is building toward a major onslaught against us. "Oh, you Christians are free to believe whatever you like, as long as you're willing to acknowledge that what everybody else believes is just as good, just as helpful. Don't you Christians know that there are a thousand different roads all going to the same place?" Of course, we believe that. It's just that the thousand different roads are all going to hell.

A Christian Defense of Christ

Christians are compelled by the Savior to say there is only one road to heaven. There is only One who may say, "I am the way, and the truth, and the life. No one comes to the Father except through me" (John 14:6). Notice that Christians did not invent this exclusivist language. These are the words of the Savior, and this is why the Savior had to say, "Blessed is the one who is not offended by me." He says, in essence, "I know your life would be easier if I weren't so demanding of your exclusive loyalty, but blessed is the one who is not offended by me."

What should we think about these charges brought against Christianity, brought against monotheism, and brought against Christ? Should we think that it is Christianity and religions like Christianity, which are exclusive in their claim, that cause so much trouble, so much bigotry, and so much violence in this world? What are we to think of these charges?

The first thing we, as Christians, ought always to say in our defense of Christ is that we are not really defending ourselves. We are not making any claims about our universal goodness. We are not insisting that Christians have not, often in the history of mankind, been guilty of grievous sins. We need to be as open and clear about that as we can. Christians, sometimes out of good motives and sometimes out of bad motives, have done terrible things.

Christians have been racists, a sin we need to acknowledge, seeking the mercy of God while doing whatever we can to make restitution. Christians have been anti-intellectual and bigoted in their ways of thinking, and we don't have to make any apology for that, but we should recognize and confess it. Sometimes, in the name of Christ, in the history of the church, Christians have been violent, usually through a misunderstanding of the proper relationship of church and state, but nonetheless they have done violence.

Today then when Muslims say, "There was horrible slaughter at the hands of Crusaders," we ought to say it is true, and that we abhor it. We acknowledge the sinfulness of it, and we are grieved by it. But we ought also to say without defensiveness or arrogance that the charge that monotheism is causing the problems in this world is simply not true.

This is not, of course, to say that some Christian monotheisms haven't caused problems in the history of the world and done terribly wrong things. But the charge that monotheism at its core must necessarily do these things is simply wrong, and we are right to request a little honesty.

Fundamentalism

There is very little honesty about Christianity, especially in the secular media. Consider what reporters do with the word *fundamentalism*. "Oh, you know those fundamentalists—what a violent lot!" However many Christian violent whackos there have been in the last century, it nevertheless is true that Christian fundamentalism is not a violent form of religion.

Recently I read a review of a church history book that was commended for exposing fundamentalists in the nineteenth century. This is a scholarly book, well reviewed, put out by a scholarly publisher. The only problem with the book is that there were no fundamentalists in the nineteenth century. Fundamentalism is a twentieth-century word. *Fundamentalism* is a word used to describe those folk who, in the early part of the twentieth century, said they believed in the fundamentals of the Christian faith. It had nothing to do with terrorism or violence. It had to do with Christians saying Christians really ought to believe in the physical resurrection of Jesus Christ. Christians really ought to believe in miracles. Christians ought to believe in the inspiration of Scripture. Christians ought to believe in the substitutionary atonement. These fundamentalists were devout preachers and serious theologians who wrote pamphlets in defense of these things called *The Fundamentals*. They stood against those who call themselves modernists who wanted the church to get with it. The fundamentalists said, "No, we don't want to be 'with it.' We want to be faithful. We want to hold to the foundational truths of the Christian faith."

It is sad and objectionable that somehow this good word has been changed and distorted to a word that now applies to any sort of way-out, violent group. When it comes to this matter of violence, when the secularists and the neopagans speak smugly to us about how we should eschew this religion that leads to so much violence, we ought to ask, "Who are the most violent in human history?" If you take all the people killed by Christians, Jews, and Muslims and added them up together, they would not begin to approach the number of people killed by atheists and neopagans in the twentieth century in the name of fascism and communism.

The most violent are those who believe in the survival of the fittest. After all, how does a Darwinist avoid the conclusions that Adolf Hitler reached? If the weak are going to be killed off by nature, why not aid nature in the process? One of the first things Adolf Hitler did when he came to power was to begin euthanizing disabled German children. How, if you believe in Darwinism, can you criticize him for that? Ideas have consequences, and these consequences seemed in the minds of many in the twentieth century to be scientific and idealistic. Both Nazism and communism in their own perverted ways were idealistic, leading to the death of millions and millions and millions—numbers that we'll probably never really fully know.

Christian Guilt

Christians, too, bear a great measure of guilt for things done in the history of mankind. But let's have a little fairness in this process. Let's have a little accuracy in this discussion. In point of fact, Christianity has been much more a protector than an oppressor, for all its faults in the history of the church.

Even when it comes to Christian relations with Islam, while sincerely apologizing for the Crusades we should remind our Muslim friends that in 1453 (not so very long ago for a church historian!) Constantinople, today known as Istanbul, was a Christian city. It had been a Christian city for 1,100 years, and the Muslim Sultan Mehmet II attacked the city with some 200,000 troops when it was being defended by about 10,000 Christian defenders. Even with such an army, he still wouldn't have taken the city (it was so marvelously defended by its walls) except that Mehmet had been able to buy a lot of huge cannons forged by Christians in Europe, and with those cannons, he knocked down the defenses of Constantinople and took the city.

Istanbul has been a Muslim city for almost 600 years, but it was a Christian city for 1,100 years. Earlier, what is today Turkey had been Christian; Syria had been Christian; Lebanon had been Christian; Egypt had been Christian; and North Africa had been Christian. Who attacked whom initially? Again, the point is not that we want Constantinople back. We certainly do not want a holy war between the two religions. Both the Christian Crusaders and the Muslim invaders misunderstood a proper relationship between church and state. But there ought to be some factuality of the accounting of these things.

Most importantly, Christians must not to allow the naysayers and the critics to diminish for a moment our commitment to saying that Jesus is Lord. His is the name that is above every name. If you do not acknowledge that name, if you do not find refuge in him, there is no hope for this life or the life of the world to come. We, as Christians, have to be willing to take that offense upon ourselves. We need to find ways to testify to the uniqueness and absolute necessity of knowing Jesus Christ—not arrogantly, nor proudly, as we are prone to, but faithfully—so that the Savior never comes to one of us and says "Why were you offended by me?"

Offended by the Cross of Christ

Then, of course, there are the folks who are not just offended by the Christ of the cross but are also offended by the cross of the Christ. The heart of the offense of the cross of Christ is summed up briefly in one of our hymns: "Jesus paid it all, all to Him I owe." This strikes at the heart of all our human pride, all our conventional human wisdom, all our insistence that surely our work must count for something. Surely we must make some contribution to our own salvation. The cross of Christ stands before us all to say that we are helpless, hopeless, dead, and unable to save ourselves. We must trust the full and complete work of Jesus Christ.

Paul develops this truth in Philippians 3:5–6 by sharing a bit of his personal history. He writes that he was "circumcised on the eighth day, of the people of Israel, of the tribe of Benjamin, a Hebrew of Hebrews; as to the law, a Pharisee; as to zeal, a persecutor of the church; as to righteousness under the law, blameless." Adding up all of his religious assets, Paul says, "If anyone else thinks he has reason for confidence in the flesh, I have more" (3:4).

Perhaps he has in mind those Philippians who were proud of their special status in the Roman Empire. They were citizens of Rome, and Romans were very proud of their empire, with its wisdom, the justice of its laws, and its kindness to inferior people. Paul is probably saying here, as the New Testament says over and over, "If you think you're something because of your blood, because of your education, because of your acquired holiness, because of your wealth, because of your wisdom, it doesn't measure up at all to what I have."

If there was ever anyone who could boast in his blood, it was Paul. He knew his tribe, and he knew the faithfulness of his devotion to the law. He says that if we think we have acquired any wisdom or any holiness in our lives, it doesn't begin to measure up to what he had in Judaism, in his devotion to the law. When Paul says we cannot be saved by works of the law, he insists that we cannot be saved by the very best things that could possibly be done by human beings.

The Cross and "Works of the Law"

There are many commentators in the history of the church who have tried to reduce "works of the law" to some kind of inferior working. This completely misunderstands Paul's point. Works of the law are the best kind of working there can be because such works are according to the law that God has revealed. Paul is saying, "If I, as one of the chosen people, have to say I count it all as loss, how much more must you say that about whatever it is you take pride in?"

That is why there are enemies of the cross. The cross insists on our self-humiliation; it insists that we recognize how weak, how lost, how helpless we are, which is hard for all of us to swallow. Paul says the only hope is that Jesus came that he might give us a righteousness that we would never have in or accomplish for ourselves. Paul declares that his hope is to be found in Christ, "not having a righteousness of my own that comes from the law, but that which comes through faith in Christ, the righteousness from God that depends on faith" (Phil. 3:9). That is our hope. That is our glory. That is our confession. Christ's righteousness, not my own, and if I want to add to Christ's righteousness, then I have offended him. I am offended to think he had to do it all and there is nothing that I have to do.

The truth is that whenever we try to add to the righteousness of Christ, we take away from it. A dear friend who was my pastor for fifteen years gave an illustration: "Think for a minute of Leonardo da Vinci's great painting, *Mona Lisa*. Now add a moustache." Addition can be subtraction. That is what happens whenever we want to add to the perfection of Christ's righteousness. Our little efforts are not an addition.

This highlights the importance of a much-assailed doctrine: the active obedience of Christ, the great Christian truth that Christ fully kept the law in our place and that his obedience in keeping the law is imputed to us through faith. The good news of the gospel is not just that Jesus takes away our sin, but also that he gives us his righteousness so that we may be able to stand accepted before God because his righteousness has been imputed to us. When we realize that we, as sinners, have nothing to contribute to our righteousness, except for sin, we will crave that righteousness that is credited to us through faith in Jesus. But Paul here makes more of Christ's passive obedience, that he was crucified for us to bear our sins. This is a constant theme in his writings: "I decided to know nothing among you except Jesus Christ and him crucified" (1 Cor. 2:2).

Why Paul Stresses the Cross

Why does Paul speak that way? He underscores and stresses the cross because it is so surprising, so unlikely, and so contrary to human wisdom that the eternal Son of Glory should die for sinners. The fact that Christ keeps the law is really not so surprising, but that he should die for sinners is amazing, isn't it? Is it possible that as long-time Christians we have become desensitized as to how amazing this is?

When you think about your own sin, how can it be that God made his sinless Son—the eternal one, the one who for all eternity had known only goodness and glory and light—"sin who knew no sin, so that in him we might become the righteousness of God" (2 Cor. 5:21)? That is truly staggering. The world opposes this claim because it so undermines all of our claims to goodness and self-assertion—all of what we would like to think about ourselves.

But the cross of Christ is not only offensive because it humiliates us and gives all the glory to Christ and his saving work on the cross; it is also offensive, Paul points out, because the cross by the work of Christ creates a new people. Part of the offense of the cross is Christ's declaration that the cross divides all of mankind into two halves, those who are redeemed in Christ and those who are outside of him. It is a terrible offense of the cross to say that the great division of mankind is not the division between one race or another, or the division between male and female, or the division between rich and poor, or the division between educated and uneducated; the great division is between those who are regenerated in Christ and those who remain his unregenerate enemies. Paul describes that difference very tellingly.

Enemies of the Cross

What are the enemies of the cross like? Paul says in Philippians 3:19 that "their end is destruction, their god is their belly, and they glory in their shame, with minds set on earthly things." It's not surprising that the enemies of the cross are upset to be described in that way, but Paul says it is the truth. We can say four things about the enemies of the cross, in contrast to those who take refuge through faith in Christ's offensive blood.

First, their end is destruction. But what is our end? Philippians 3:20 answers, "Our citizenship is in heaven." This is what characterizes those who have taken refuge in the cross—not destruction and death but an eternal weight of glory that fades not away, an eternal life of blessedness that comes to us from the Savior.

Second, their god is their belly. Paul probably means more here than just Gentile excess of self-indulgence; he is likely including even Jewish concentration on dietary laws and all sorts of visible things that tie us to this world. Our God is a Savior that we await from heaven, the Lord Jesus Christ, the Jesus whom we don't see now, whose timetable still seems a very strange one, who allows things to happen to his people in this world that seem so troubling and unaccountable. Paul says when you are suffering in this world, look up and remember you have a Savior, the Lord Jesus Christ. Though we do not see him now, and although we must live by faith now, he is coming. He is coming again.

Third, the glory of the enemies of the cross is their shame; that is, they glory in things they know are wrong. We all have a moral law deeply rooted in our souls that, at some level, we cannot deny. Saint Augustine gave great expression to this when he quipped, "No thief is so immoral that he does not object to being stolen from." There is a moral reality that causes shame, even in the hearts of the enemies of God.

But believers, far from glorying in their shame, glory in the promise (Phil. 3:21) that Jesus is going to transform our lowly bodies, still too often bound up in sin, to be like his glorious body. There is a day coming when he will take away all the power, reality, and presence of sin within us, and we will be holy as he is holy. We will be righteous as he is righteous because we will have been transformed.

Fourth, the enemies of the cross set their minds on earthly things, things that pass away, things that Psalm 49 reminds us we can't take with us. Pharaoh tried to take what he had with him. He was buried with mountains of gold, but within generations grave robbers had bored through the tons of rock to steal the gold. You really can't take it with you. This world sets its mind on earthly things, but Christians set their minds on the power that enables Jesus even to subject all things to himself.

There is a God. There is a God who is in charge of this world. There is a God who does all things well. There is a God who is bringing his elect to glory. There is a God who is building his church. Sometimes we wonder, when the church seems weak and frail, if God couldn't be doing this a little more gloriously. Why can't we see thousands and millions coming to faith instead of only a trickle?

Of course, sometimes we are looking in the wrong place. Just one example is what occurred in Reformed and Presbyterian missions in the twentieth century. Hundreds of thousands were brought to faith in Nigeria by Reformed missions. In Korea, perhaps millions were brought to faith by Presbyterian missions. God is still at work, transforming things in this world and bringing people to life. Although we wish we didn't have to go on suffering, Paul said that our suffering completes "what is lacking in Christ's afflictions" (Col.

1:24). What can that mean? While his church goes on suffering, the day of salvation continues in this world. The enemies of Christ can hear the gospel, and enemies of the cross, as Paul once was, can be converted.

Blessed in Christ

"Blessed is the one who is not offended by me." Let us have confidence in our Savior. Let us have confidence in the Christ of the cross and in the cross of the Christ. Let us assert that Jesus knows what he is doing and that we want to serve him according to his Word. Then let us follow the model that Paul has set for us in Philippians 3, that when we think of the enemies of the cross, we think of them with tears: "For many, of whom I have often told you and now tell you even with tears, walk as enemies of the cross of Christ" (v. 18).

It is easy to think of these enemies with hatred or arrogance. It is easy to despise them. But let's think of unbelievers with grief in our hearts. There are so many who do not know the Savior, and as Christ was not offended by sinners but sought to draw them to himself, let us, as the people of God, with tears in our eyes, turn again and again to the enemies of Christ. Let us tell them, "There is life for you in him. There is mercy for you in his cross. Come to the Savior now." For blessed is everyone who is not offended in him.

PRECIOUS BLOOD

R. C. Sproul

You were ransomed from the futile ways inherited from your forefathers, not with perishable things such as silver or gold, but with the precious blood of Christ, like that of a lamb without blemish or spot.

—1 Peter 1:18–19

Like people, words can be either dignified or undignified depending on the company they keep. Take the word *precious*. It has not helped that a woman named Patti Williams took the name Precious for her onscreen antics alongside her professional wrestling husband, Gorgeous Jimmy Garvin. Quite a bit better is the tendency of mothers to describe their newborn babies as precious. But the word *precious* also keeps the most exalted company in all of history, since the atoning blood of God's own Son is described in the Bible with this word. When the apostle Peter writes to remind the early Christians that they were not redeemed with common, perishable things, he states that it was with the "precious blood of Christ" that they were redeemed.

This lexical survey reminds us that we need to give some effort to understanding the actual meaning assigned to words in the Bible. As we think about Christ's *precious* blood, I want to consider its biblical meaning and also why the apostle Peter would use an adjective of this type to describe the atoning blood of our Lord. What is it, we should ask, that makes the blood of Christ precious?

Flawlessly Precious

Let's begin with a brief look at the word *precious*. We know that something precious transcends the ordinary, the commonplace, and brings us into the realm of the uncommon and the extraordinary. For instance, we all know that in the land around us, we find a multitude of stones and rocks that are, for the most part, somewhat useless and, at times, even represent an impediment, particularly to the farmer when he seeks to plant his crops. He must first go through the arduous task of removing the stones from the land; he knows that when he sows the seed for his crops, if the seed falls upon the stones, it cannot germinate and bring any root. So these common stones are often considered merely a waste.

But we also know that there are other stones that are more rare and more scarce, and in some instances quite beautiful. These stones have a certain commercial value, and we refer to them as gemstones. But there is a category even higher than that when we use the term *precious* to describe certain stones. Some stones have an exceedingly high value, precious stones such as diamonds, rubies, and emeralds.

On our twenty-fifth wedding anniversary, I wanted to honor my wife of a quarter century. I happened to have a friend in Orlando who had a jeweler friend in New York City who was a noted gemologist. So I asked my friend, "Can you find a way to secure for me a wonderful diamond that I could give to Vesta for our twenty-fifth anniversary?"

My friend contacted the jeweler in New York City, a man in his seventies who had been in the practice for over fifty years. After a while, I got the report that he had found a stone he believed was suitable for this new engagement ring that I was going to give my wife. He made a trip to Orlando to show it to me. It was wrapped in tissue paper, and he opened up the paper and said, "I want to tell you a story about this stone. I've been a jeweler for over fifty years, and it's been my task to rate and evaluate diamonds according to their color, beauty, and flaws."

He went on, "Never in my practice have I rated a diamond as flawless. But for the first time in my practice, I have found a diamond in which I have not been able to detect a single flaw, and here it is. Still," he continued, "I have to tell you I haven't rated it as flawless. I rated it as museum quality, but not as flawless, because I don't think there is such thing as a flawless stone. Even though I can't find the flaw, there has to be one there."

This was just what I wanted for my wife. So I told her about the stone and felt pretty good about myself when I gave it to her for our twenty-fifth anniversary.

When I look at that diamond, I am reminded that while some things may appear to be flawless, there is only one who is truly flawless. And when Peter assigns the word *precious* to the blood of Jesus, it's because the blood of Jesus is the blood of a person who really was flawless. What makes the atoning sacrifice of Jesus valuable is that it was offered by one who was sinless. It was offered by one who was a lamb without blemish, without flaw. And Jesus' blood had to be flawless, because anything less would not do.

I have always been surprised at where the liberal critics of the Christian faith aim their guns. They tend to focus on the miracles of Jesus and particularly on the resurrection or the virgin birth of Christ. "Oh, come on now," they say, "the virgin birth goes against all nature, all science. It couldn't have happened, and when people die, we all know that they stay dead, so the idea of a resurrection is a myth." But I wonder why they spend so much attention on the supernatural nature of Christ rather than on the extraordinary aspect of his sinlessness. Is there anything more rare, more scarce, more extraordinary? Is there anything more uncommon than a human being without sin? Is there anything more precious? Of course, if we understand that death is a consequence of sin, we can understand easily that one who was sinless was raised from the dead. What is truly amazing about the Gospel accounts is that death held Jesus at all, in light of his flawlessly precious character.

Precious to Redeem

When Peter speaks of the "precious blood" of Jesus, he is referring to the value of the blood. I have found that Christians often ask what it was about the blood of Jesus that saves us. Was there some kind of magical power inherent in the blood that went through his veins? Didn't our salvation require Jesus' life and not just his blood?

Many years ago, my friend John Guest raised this question: If Jesus came down from heaven and scratched his finger on a nail, would that have done it? There would have been blood and it would have been the blood of Jesus; wouldn't that have been enough to redeem our souls? Of course the answer to that question is no. If Jesus scratched his finger on a nail, he would have survived it. He would not have died. He would not have been put to death. He would not have given his life. It is Christ's precious person that is symbolized by his blood.

I thought about that question for many, many years: If Jesus scratched his finger on a nail, would it have been enough to save us? In terms of what God requires to cover our sins, obviously the theological answer is no, it would not be enough. "The wages of sin is death" (Rom. 6:23), so Jesus had to die for us. Yet, when I contemplate Jesus spilling one drop of blood for me, just one scratch on his finger, it would seem to be so valuable that I really think it would be enough to pay for my sins, because of the great chasm that exists between the flaws of my life and the perfection of his. For a perfect man to shed one drop for me is more than I'll ever be able to understand in this world. That blood is flawless.

Again, if Jesus had one flaw, committed one sin, a single peccadillo, a tiny sin, an inconsequential sin, he would have been disqualified to be our Savior because God required the sacrifice that was without blemish. So it is because Jesus in his holy perfection is precious that his blood is precious to redeem. The Bible speaks about our redemption in terms of a purchase. The apostle Paul said to his people, "You are not your own, for you were bought with a price" (1 Cor. 6:19–20). What does that mean—you are not your own? You might say, "Of course, I'm my own. Who else's am I? I'm free. I don't belong to anybody else." But Paul said, "Oh, yes, you do. You are not your own because you have been bought. You have been purchased. You have been bought and you have been paid for, and the price that was paid was the blood of Jesus."

Now, dear reader, how much are you worth? Our creditors ask us this all the time. What is your net worth? How valuable are you? What was Jesus getting at when he said to those who were around him, "For what will it profit a man if he gains the whole world and forfeits his soul?" (Matt. 16:26). When Jesus weighed that economic transition, he obviously meant that the worth of the whole world cannot compare to the value of your soul. He went on to ask, "Or what shall a man give in return for his soul?" (Matt. 16:26).

We hear the cynical wisdom that every man has his price. What's your price? How much would you take in exchange for your soul? But at no time in history has such a premium been put on the value of your soul than when Jesus paid for your soul with the purchase of his own precious blood.

Precious in Heaven

We can consider how much the blood of Christ is worth to us. It is worth our salvation. It is worth eternity for us. But how valuable was the blood of Jesus to God the Father? How much worth did the Father place on his Son?

Three times in the New Testament we have a record of God speaking audibly from heaven. When God speaks audibly from heaven in the New Testament, the message is basically the same. He points to

Jesus, and he says, "This is my beloved Son." He could have said,
"This is my precious son. This is my valued son. This is my beloved
Son, my cherished son, in whom I am well pleased." On one occasion, the Father said, "This is my beloved Son, with whom I am well
pleased; listen to him" (Matt. 17:5). How could any human being
not value the words of Jesus? What human being could lightly dismiss the living Word of God (John 1:1), upon whom God puts the
supreme value and calls him *precious*?

A thorough study of the atonement will have to consider the
ways in which Jesus fulfilled the messianic prophecy of the Suffering
Servant, presented so brilliantly in Isaiah 53. "Surely he has borne
our griefs and carried our sorrows," Isaiah writes (53:4). "He was
wounded for our transgressions; he was crushed for our iniquities"
(v. 5). These are familiar statements, but there is a line that baffles
us or, to use the contemporary jargon, "boggles the mind." When
the prophet is speaking the Word of God, listen to what he says: "It
was the will of the LORD to crush him" (v. 10). I like the stronger
language of the King James Version: "Yet it pleased the LORD to
bruise him."

Who can get their arms around that? How can it please God to
bruise his only begotten Son in whom he himself is well pleased?
Doesn't that seem like a radical conflict of pleasure? How could God
take pleasure in the pain of his Son? How can the Bible say by divine
inspiration that it pleased the Lord to bruise him? To understand
that, we have to go not only back to the prophet Isaiah, but also
back to eternity before the prophet even spoke, back to eternity when
the Father and the Son and the Holy Ghost agreed on God's eternal
plan to redeem a fallen race and where God the Father sovereignly
decreed that our redemption would be accomplished through the
sacrificial death of his Son.

In eternity past, we see in the counsel of God that he so loved
the world that he would give that gift which was most supremely
precious. It was not because God took delight in inflicting pain upon

his Son in some sadistic cosmic form of child abuse. The only reason the atoning work of the Son pleased the Father was that he knew that by his Son's bruises that you and I would be healed.

The bruises of Jesus are precious in the sight of the Father, and not only in the sight of the Father, but also in the sight of the whole host of heaven. This is why one of my favorite texts in all the New Testament is found in Revelation 5. Before I reveal it, I need to give you some background from Revelation 4. There John says, "After this I looked, and behold, a door standing open in heaven! And the first voice, which I had heard speaking to me like a trumpet, said, 'Come up here, and I will show you what must take place after this'" (Rev. 4:1). God pulled away the veil so that the apostle could see into heaven. John was in exile on the island of Patmos, and God said to him, "John, I'm going to let you peek into the inner sanctum of heaven itself." So John writes:

> At once I was in the Spirit, and behold, a throne stood in heaven, with one seated on the throne. And he who sat there had the appearance of jasper and carnelian, and around the throne was a rainbow that had the appearance of an emerald. Around the throne were twenty-four thrones, and seated on the thrones were twenty-four elders, clothed in white garments, with golden crowns on their heads. From the throne came flashes of lightning, and rumblings and peals of thunder, and before the throne were burning seven torches of fire, which are the seven spirits of God, and before the throne there was as it were a sea of glass, like crystal. (Rev. 4:2–6)

Let's now move on to Revelation 5. John has given us the initial glimpse into heaven, where he sees the throne of God with all of its glory and majesty, and then in chapter 5 he says, "I saw in the right hand of him who was seated on the throne a scroll written within and on the back, sealed with seven seals" (v. 1). The scroll was sealed and shut and locked from view, not with one seal but with seven seals. It was sealed as tightly as it could be, kept hidden from the gaze of any creature and from the view of any human being. John trembles in excitement when he sees this scroll, the mystery of the ages contained inside.

He continues, "I saw a strong angel proclaiming with a loud voice, 'Who is worthy to open the scroll and break its seals?'" (v. 2). John hears this announcement, this question, "Who is worthy?" In anticipation, he looks around the scene of heaven, and he waits for a worthy one to step forward to open this sealed book.

First there's the joy of anticipation, then a moment of consternation because, in horror, John writes, "And no one in heaven or on earth or under the earth was able to open the scroll or to look into it" (v. 3). Listen as he describes his response. Does John say, "I began to weep. I began to have tears trickle down my cheek as I softly wept in disappointment"? No, he writes, "I began to weep loudly because no one was found worthy to open the scroll or to look into it" (v. 4). He is sobbing, beloved. Why? Because no one was found worthy to open the scroll or even to look at it. But suddenly one of the elders said, "Weep no more; behold, the Lion of the tribe of Judah, the Root of David, has conquered, so that he can open the scroll and its seven seals" (v. 5).

John's manifold disappointment instantly changes into radical excitement. He can't wait for the entrance of the Lion of Judah who will step forward and grab that scroll and, with the power of his claws, rip open the seals and expose this holy book. John looks expectantly for the lion. Then he tells us, "Between the throne and the four living creatures and among the elders I saw a Lamb standing." A lamb, not a lion, and not just an ordinary lamb—not a common lamb, but a lamb standing "as though it had been slain." It was "with seven horns and with seven eyes, which are the seven spirits of God sent out into all the earth" (v. 6).

This Lamb that was slain then took the scroll from the right hand of him who was seated on the throne. And when he had taken the scroll, the four living creatures and the twenty-four elders fell on their knees before the Lamb. Each one was holding a harp and golden balls full of incense, which are the prayers of the saints, and they started to sing.

We know from the Old Testament that when God accomplishes victory over the enemies of his people, the people of God under the inspiration of the Spirit compose a song of deliverance. At the Red Sea parting, Moses and the Israelites sang: "I will sing to the LORD, for he has triumphed gloriously; the horse and his rider he has thrown into the sea" (Ex. 15:1). Deborah sang, "From heaven the stars fought, from their courses they fought against Sisera" (Judg. 5:20).

Again and again we see this phenomenon. We see a concentration of such singing in the early infancy narratives of the birth of our Lord, particularly in Luke's Gospel. We see the Benedictus of Zechariah: "Blessed be the Lord God of Israel, for he has visited and redeemed his people" (Luke 1:68). We sing the Magnificat of Mary: "My soul magnifies the Lord, and my spirit rejoices in God my Savior" (Luke 1:46–47). Simeon sang the Nunc Dimittus when he beheld the Messiah, brought to the temple for his dedication: "Lord, now you are letting your servant depart in peace, according to your word; for my eyes have seen your salvation" (Luke 2:29–30).

Now let's go back to the book of Revelation. Does not God tell us there that he will give to his people a new song? I think we get a glimpse of what that new song will sound like when we read of this song that is composed in heaven, when the Lamb who was slain prevails to open up the book, and they sang a new song. Listen to the words:

> "Worthy are you to take the scroll and to open its seals, for you were slain, and by your blood you ransomed people for God from every tribe and language and people and nation, and you have made them a kingdom and priests to our God, and they shall reign on the earth." (Rev. 5:9–10)

John says, "Then I looked, and I heard around the throne and the living creatures and the elders the voice of many angels, numbering myriads of myriads and thousands of thousands" (Rev. 5:11). Not a few angels, but myriads of myriads, thousands of thousands of angels singing with a loud voice: "Worthy is the Lamb who was slain" (v. 12).

The words could be translated, "*Precious* is the Lamb who was slain"—worthy to receive power, worthy to receive wealth and wisdom and might and honor, and glory and blessing. And then, John says, he heard every creature in heaven and every creature on earth, and every creature under the earth in the sea, and all that is in them crying out, "To him who sits on the throne and to the Lamb be blessing and honor and glory and might forever and ever!" (v. 13).

The response in heaven, I pray, is the response of everyone who considers the message of this song. For marveling with great joy at the precious blood of Christ, the four living creatures cried out before the throne of God, "Amen!" (Rev. 5:14). They cried, "Amen!" and fell down before the precious Lamb, with his precious blood, and they worshiped him.

PART 2

THE *Atonement*
IN CHRISTIAN THOUGHT

EARLY CHURCH REFLECTIONS ON THE ATONEMENT

Derek W. H. Thomas

Any discussion of the doctrine of the atonement in the early church is almost bound to be puzzling. The early centuries of the Christian church were spent almost exclusively defending biblical definitions of the person of Christ, both in relationship to the hypostatic union of the divine and human natures and to the Trinitarian relationship of Christ within the Godhead. Some formulations on the atonement are undeveloped and provisional in nature, and some, frankly, are erroneous.

But, first, we need to ask what we mean by *the early church*. We could, for example, suggest with all fairness that the early church is the church immediately following Pentecost, the church as represented in the Acts of the Apostles. In that case, we could talk about Paul's doctrine of the atonement or Peter's doctrine of the atonement and compare these categories with concepts from the sixteenth and seventeenth centuries. Or one could look at many passages in the Epistles and tease out a doctrine of the atonement. That would be perfectly legitimate.

But in referring to the early church, we are referring to something other than the apostolic age. The period in question here is what we

generally refer to as the Patristic period, a generic term that covers
the period from the apostles to the time of Constantine (he became
emperor in AD 324), and onward to the beginning of the medieval
period around AD 600.[1]

Many of our categories of theology, for good or ill, are derived
from the theological contributions and interactions of Augustine (AD
354–430). He is the great figure of early church history. We cannot
overestimate his influence on the Western church (Catholicism and
later Protestantism). B. B. Warfield famously suggested that what we
see in the Reformation is the triumph of Augustine's doctrine of grace
over his doctrine of the church.[2] In soteriological and harmartological
terms, therefore, Augustine's contribution is enormously significant.

And we cannot overlook the Eastern Church and its assessment
of the doctrine of the cross.[3] The *Christus Victor* view of the atonement, for example, though often anachronistically caricatured and
misunderstood, is something that the Eastern church has held to for
centuries in various forms.

A Work in Progress

Taken as a whole, the Patristic era utilized categories in describing
the atonement in a more or less *organic* fashion. The early church
employed a variety of biblical metaphors without stressing one in
particular or infusing theologically driven ideas or any carefully delineated insistence on pinpointing the exact location of orthodox
boundary markers. The issue here is not confined to the doctrine of
the atonement, of course. The Bible is not given to us in the form
of John Calvin's *Institutes* or Louis Berkof's *Systematic Theology*.
A Reformed doctrine of the atonement is not given to us in an ap-
pendix following the book of Revelation. But then, neither is the
doctrine of the hypostatic union or the perichoretic nature of Trinitarian fellowship. Theology must be done in a disciplined attempt
to formulate coherent, unified expressions of truth from the diverse,
organic nature of Scripture.

Theology, in particular *systematic* theology, is a correlate of the unity of Scripture. This is true despite its poly-generic nature. Scripture, for example, contains law, prophecy, epistles, love poems, proverbs, history, apocalyptic, etc. This is true also despite its organic nature. Revelation is given piecemeal, reflecting the particular period of redemptive history in which it is found. And this is true despite its multi-authored composition. "Men spoke," Peter tells us (2 Pet. 1:21), so that Paul sounds different from Peter, and Isaiah from Amos. Scripture is, nevertheless, "from God," essentially authored by one mind—God's—and having, as a result, an indigenous harmony and coherence. Systematic theology is possible because one coherent and rational mind is at work in writing Holy Scripture. But when it comes to the Patristic writings, the effort to draw forth an effective summary of the Bible's teaching of various doctrines was very much a work in the early stages of progress.

Doctrine Developed

So how does doctrine, or dogma, develop, and what is doctrine?[4] The trajectory from biblical data—individual "texts" of Scripture, including what look like embryonic doctrinal statements within the canon of Scripture itself (e.g., "Jesus is Lord," 1 Cor. 12:3)—to the codification of doctrine in ecumenical creeds and confessional standards is a fascinating study.

It is equally fascinating to note that no ecumenical creed pronounced anything of substance on the doctrine of the atonement. The Apostles' Creed, for example, says nothing beyond the fact that Jesus "suffered under Pontius Pilate, was crucified, dead, and buried." Nothing here is said on the meaning of Jesus' death as penal substitution, as a sacrifice of atonement, or as a propitiation (of God's wrath against sin), let alone a statement as to the *effectiveness* of the atonement. The Apostles' Creed makes only a general statement that faith in life everlasting is in some way dependant on his death and consequent resurrection. One could, euphemistically speaking, drive a "cart and horses" through these statements.

It is true, however, that the Apostles' Creed does seem to be alluding to the statement in the opening section of 1 Corinthians 15, where the apostle Paul writes: "I delivered to you as of first importance . . ." (v. 3). Paul is saying that there are doctrines, or truths, that are *first of all*. This implies that there are other truths that are second. There are primary truths and there are secondary truths. The death of Christ and what it means is a primary truth. We will need to be clearer as to how much of the meaning of the death of Christ is primary and how much of it is secondary.

This does not suggest, of course, that *any* truth is unimportant. The point of distinguishing between primary and secondary is to note areas without which we are not even in the realms of Christianity. According to Paul, the first of these central doctrines is the atonement. Without some statement on the cross, there is no Christianity. Yet here we should observe that we don't really get statements about the atonement in anything like a creedal form until the Reformation, and especially the great confessions of the sixteenth and seventeenth centuries.[5] The ecumenical creeds of the early church are largely concerned with the person of Christ and the doctrine of the Trinity.

Early Church Atonement Themes

It is an interesting observation, maybe a disturbing observation, that it took fifteen hundred years before the church put the doctrine of the atonement in its crosshairs. But it would be a categorical mistake to draw the conclusion that the church had no *implicit*, pre-critical view(s) on the meaning of Calvary and the empty tomb. In some form, penal substitution and its attendant categories had in fact been believed since the early church, even if it did not receive precise formulation as Christian doctrine until the sixteenth or seventeenth centuries.

We may well ask why it took that long, or why, in God's providence, the atonement was allowed to lie dormant for that length of time, but answering the question will be difficult and speculative. It is one of the mysteries of providence. Part of the answer is that truth is often formulated in creedal statements *in opposition to error*. There is a context in which these things take place. In the early church the discussions were largely on the deity of Jesus or the humanity of Jesus because there were influential people vigorously denying his humanity or his deity. Then those who confirmed both his humanity and deity were confused about the relationship of these two natures to each other. These are the issues which dominated the third, fourth, and even fifth centuries.[6]

In the second century (roughly AD 120–200), the issue that dominated the early church was the *Gnostic* issue. The whole involvement of God with creation, the relationship of spirit to matter, was under the microscope. There is the figure of Marcion, for example, who jettisoned the entirety of the Old Testament as being sub-Christian and portions of the New Testament (such as Matthew) as being too Jewish in nature.[7]

Early Christian writers were therefore mesmerized by the opening chapters of Genesis, and especially by the account of the fall. Many of the early apologists, for example, dealt largely with Gnosticism on the one hand or the Marcionite tendency on the other, to such an extent that what emerged in the second century was a view of salvation that was seen as a threefold dynamic justifying the Old Testament: God sent prophets, first of all, to instruct; he spelled out the rigors of Old Testament worship to make Israel stand out to the nations; and then the early church spent a great deal of time emphasizing the importance of the incarnation as the culmination of the Old Testament.

God's dealings with Israel, therefore, were largely seen as preparations for the coming of the Messiah, or Jesus as the covenant mediator. The chief concern then was on his *identity*: who is Jesus? Then they asked questions like, "What is significant about his Jewishness? What is new about the new covenant, and what is the relationship between that newness and the old covenant?" In addition, we can identify several broad themes that appeared.

Christ's Work

First is the theme that *Christ's work was essentially ethical and pedagogical*: Jesus was in essence a teacher and an example; he came to typify for us godliness. Jesus was seen as one who exemplified obedience to God's law. All this was done in the light of discussions in Greek philosophy, particularly in Plato and Aristotle.

The whole issue for some was ethical: Christ is the pinnacle of the godly life. One can readily imagine the situation in the early church, particularly as Bibles were scarce and often incomplete. Believers were dependent on memory and on what they had been taught, instructed, and catechized about Christ as the great example to follow. For those with Marcionite tendencies, the gospel was the "new law" in opposition to Old Testament law. By the second century, the Christian church had to defend itself not just against coexistence with Judaism, but also in opposition to Judaism. Thus Christ was set forth as the new lawgiver in the place of Moses.

The Centrality of the Cross

The second broad theme that appeared in the early church was *a pre-critical recognition of the centrality of the cross*. Special mention should be given to Irenaeus of Lyons (died ca. AD 202) and a view of the cross known as the "recapitulation theory" of the atonement.[8] There are many aspects of this view of the atonement that are biblical and orthodox. Irenaeus emphasized Jesus as a second Adam who came to repeat, repair, and recapitulate what Adam did and failed to do. Irenaeus laid great emphasis upon Christ's repairing Adam's disobedience. The tree of Adam's disobedience was repaired by the "tree" of Christ's allegiance, and the tree, of course, is the cross.[9]

Today we would want to use these biblical metaphors in a more federal/covenantal form than Irenaeus did, but essentially there is an important truth here, one that Paul expounds in Romans 5. What is it that Christ obeyed? The law! Christ obeyed a covenant of works. That language belongs in the sixteenth and seventeenth centuries and not in the second century, but the seed idea was present in Irenaeus.

Irenaeus was the first to draw comparisons between Eve and Mary, the seed of the woman. Why does Jesus, in the wedding in Cana of Galilee, say to his mother, "Woman, what does this have to do with me?" (John 2:4). You would never call your mother "Woman"! It would be enormously disrespectful in almost any society to refer to your mother as "Woman." Why, then, does Jesus call his mother "Woman"? Irenaeus's answer was that Jesus was alluding to Genesis 3 and the Mosaic words about the "seed of the woman." He is the seed of "the woman." Thus the work of Christ was seen in Adamic terms: Jesus is fulfilling what Adam failed to fulfill, providing a righteousness that was lacking in Eden. The life and death of Jesus (but especially his life) is a recapitulation of Eden.

Payment of a Ransom Price

The third broad category is the *payment of a ransom price*. Jesus said, "Even the Son of Man came not to be served but to serve, and to give his life as a ransom for many" (Mark 10:45). There seems to be no doubt that in the early church, and perhaps even as early as the late first century, this text circulated among Christians as an encapsulating or crystallizing statement. One imagines, as Christian folk met together before the New Testament had been finished, or at least before copies of it had been carefully copied and multiplied in the Roman Empire, that these would be the kinds of things they would remember by way of an oral tradition.

Jesus said he had come to give his life as a ransom for many. The question then arises, to whom are ransoms paid? The answer is to *bad* people: thieves, murderers, and terrorists.

Governments, past and present, agonize over such things as ransom payments. They always deny it, but many capitulate and pay ransoms to terrorists. Ransoms are paid to wicked people. So to whom did Jesus pay a ransom? Of course, the orthodox and biblical answer that you and I ought to say is "to God." God's wrath needs to be propitiated. His justice needs to be vindicated. Our debt to his law needs to be paid. In the second century the view developed that this ransom was paid not to God but to the Devil. Satan is, after all, the archetypal *bad* person.

From this developed a fairly pronounced view of the atonement that would largely dominate the early church right up until the period of Augustine, the so-called *Christus Victor* view.[10] More recently it has been popularized alluding in the main to its articulation by the Swedish theologian, Gustav Aulén (1879–1977).[11]

Theopoiesis

The fourth area of atonement language employed generally in the early church is that known as *theopoiesis*. This is a very technical term of enormous significance in Eastern Orthodox theology.[12] The term is loosely rendered "divinization," but that is far too simplistic. It takes a more or less literal rendition of 2 Peter 1:4, "You may become partakers of the divine nature." This is one of those texts surrounded by a thousand pitfalls. Move in any direction and you are probably doomed to commit some kind of heresy!

At the risk of oversimplification, we should ask, in union with Christ, are we sharing in the divine nature of God, and if so, in what sense? In an *analogical* sense, perhaps? There have been movements in more recent times suggesting something similar to this. One thinks of the theology of the German theologian Wolfhart Pannenburg (b. 1928), one of the great liberal voices of the late twentieth century, who essentially advocated a pantheistic view of God. Everything, in the end, becomes an extension of God, which he based on Paul's words in 1 Corinthians 15: in the end God will be "all in all" (v. 28). Reformed theology insists on the Creator-creature distinction both here and now *and* in the life to come. That distinction is not just a temporary aspect of our existence.

Nor is Irenaeus alone in his view of *theopoiesis*. Athanasius, one of the great heroes of the church as far as defending a biblical view of the deity of Christ, also entered these waters. He said that the Word "was made man so that we might be made God." These extraordinary words need to be understood within a very specific context, and it would be more than possible to make these words mean more than they intended. But it is clear that this view (*theosis* or *theopoiesis*) has greatly influenced views of the nature of what Christ did on the cross and has fundamentally addressed the relationship between the cross and what Christ achieved in his incarnation (clearly, an important issue for Athanasius).[13]

Recapitulation and Ransom Theories

Returning to the recapitulation view advocated by Irenaeus and others, we will now examine it in some greater detail. In his *Adversus Haereses* (*Against Heresies*), his magnum opus, Irenaeus spoke of Christ uniting himself with us in the incarnation in order that "we might become what he is." In the incarnation, he united himself to humanity, and so his divinity touches humanity and brings it to God. The philosophical background for Irenaeus includes a pronounced dualism in which God and Satan, good and evil, are viewed as equally ultimate and powerful. Adam had lost the battle, and good had therefore succumbed to the power of evil. On the other hand, Jesus had won the battle against the forces of darkness. This obedience is for Irenaeus a crucial issue. Christ won the victory over Satan by being obedient.

The recapitulation theory and the ransom theory overlap. In the ransom theory, a view held by Origen (the man to whom we often attribute the excessive use of typology in the Scriptures), there is an ethical dualism involving the concurrent influences of God and Satan, good and evil. The Devil holds humanity in his grasp, demanding a ransom price. And the ransom price is the death of Jesus. Jesus agrees that this price be paid, and the Devil kills him on the cross. But then, like the Trojan horse, from "inside" the tomb he emerges. The resurrected Christ appears and Satan has been duped! Satan thinks he has won. He thinks he has triumphed, but all along he has been duped, because inside the Trojan horse of the body of Jesus there is his Spirit; there is his divine nature, and Satan had not bargained for that.

Important for the ransom theory is the divine nature of Jesus. Not all agree in the early church as to whether that divine nature is part of his being or essence (that Jesus always was divine) or whether that divine nature is something that is adopted by an earthly Jesus (or vice versa). They are not all orthodox on that issue. But they all agree on the idea of paying a ransom price to the Devil. And in the face of this evil, Christ emerges as the victor (*Christus Victor*). Christ is the hero who comes back from a famous battle against a hostile and powerful enemy in glorious triumph.

There is much that is true in this view, not least the understanding that Christ is ultimately triumphant over the powers of darkness. It is a view that takes seriously, very seriously, the powers of darkness in the world. But it is a view that requires enormous care in its expression and use, and as often understood by the early church, it is a view that seriously distorts the biblical data. The Bible does not advocate an ultimate dualism. Satan is a finite being. He is a more malevolent being than you and I can imagine, but he is a finite being for all that. He cannot be in two places at the same time. So when we think that Satan is attacking us, he probably is not doing so directly. He has a host of minions that do his work, but his power is limited.

It doesn't equal the power of God, and his rule does not compare to the sovereignty of God.

Not only is the dualism of the ransom theory a problem, but so also is its ethical dimension, involving a view that basically suggests a deception. At its most blatant, it is a lie. It is one thing to suggest that there are ethical situations that necessitate us to lie, for example, when Nazi soldiers in World War II asked Christians for the location of hidden Jews. It is quite another to suggest that this forms part of God's strategy in the atonement. The problem with the ransom theory is that it involves at its very core a divine deception. You may say it is fine to deceive the Devil, and many would be sympathetic to that. And some have argued that there is a difference between a deception and an outright lie. If Satan is stupid enough to believe that Jesus is not divine, that is his fault. Nonetheless, the ransom theory involves God in what is essentially a breach of contract.

Jesus is a victor! He has entered into battle against the strong man, to use the language of Scripture, and has bound him (Mark 3:27). "[God] disarmed the rulers and authorities and put them to open shame, by triumphing over them in him" (Col. 2:15). This biblical testimony goes hand in hand with strong assertions as to the reality of Satan's power. A slithering serpent in Genesis becomes the devouring red dragon in Revelation 12, a dragon that is overthrown by the blood of the Lamb (Rev. 12:7–17).

The idea that Satan and the powers of evil must be taken into consideration in the atonement is perfectly biblical. It is a theme of the atonement. God *is* involved in a battle against the forces of darkness and opposition; but is it the main feature of the atonement? And is it to be portrayed in terms similar to those in which Irenaeus and Athanasius portrayed it?

If not to Satan then to whom is the ransom paid? Who is it that needs to be satisfied? The answer that Reformed theological reflection has given is that the one needing to be satisfied is God—in particular, the justice of God. It took the medieval period to bring this to the surface in the monumental discussions of Anselm of Canterbury and Abelard (see chapter 8 in this volume). It takes a feudal system of societal law for that to be embedded within Christian consciousness.

Penal Substitution

So is there no connection in the early church with the Reformation doctrine of penal substitutionary atonement? The answer is that the early church reveals strands of truth that later will become more refined. There are, in fact, clear pronouncements as to the penal substitutionary nature of the death of Christ on behalf of sinners. John Chrysostom (AD 347–407), Archbishop of Constantinople, for example, known to the Christian church as a great preacher and liturgist of the Eastern church, made the following statement in one of his sermons on 2 Corinthians 5:

> If one that was himself a king, beholding a robber and malefactor under punishment, gave his well-beloved son, his only-begotten and true, to be slain; and transferred the death and the guilt as well, from him to his son, (who was himself of no such character,) that he might both save the condemned man and clear him from his evil reputation; and then if, having subsequently promoted him to great dignity, he had yet, after thus saving him and advancing him to that glory unspeakable, been outraged by the person that had received such treatment: would not that man, if he had any sense, have chosen ten thousand deaths rather than appear guilty of so great ingratitude? This then let us also now consider with ourselves, and groan bitterly for the provocations we have offered our Benefactor; nor let us therefore presume, because though outraged He bears it with long-suffering; but rather for this very reason be full of remorse.[14]

It is clear that Chrysostom is employing the categories of penal substitution in order to describe the nature of the atonement. His statement could have come from Anselm or one of the Puritans! So the language of penal substitution is certainly there in the early church, but it was only one of many ways of trying to describe the nature of the death of Jesus. Within the recapitulation theory or within the ransom theory or even within the *theosis* theory, there were strands of truth. Some emphasized one aspect more than others, but there is an antiquity to the multifaceted nature of Jesus' work that finds reflection in penal substitution, satisfaction—also in terms of Christ's victory over the Evil One—and in terms of bringing us into union and fellowship with God whereby we share in his communicable attributes. That clarity on the atonement came in the medieval and Reformation periods is beyond dispute. But the preaching of the cross of Jesus Christ was also a mark of the early church.

Summary

In summary, therefore, as we noted earlier, the early church employed a variety of biblical metaphors without stressing one in particular or infusing theologically driven ideas or any carefully delineated insistence on where the boundaries lay, something which later periods of the church did, employing creedal and confessional statements to disclose the line of orthodoxy. It would be a mistake, therefore, to ignore the developmental nature of theological formulation, just as it would be to ignore the roots from which such deliberations emerged.

THE MEDIEVAL ACHIEVEMENT:
ANSELM ON THE ATONEMENT

Philip Graham Ryken

Anselm of Canterbury was one of the best theologians in the history of the church—a man of deep personal piety who pursued doctrinal clarity with painstaking care, and who made a central contribution to our understanding of the atonement—that precious blood. We know a good deal about the man because one of his contemporaries wrote his biography. This was not uncommon in those days. Someone would follow a great man of God around, looking for the miracles that would make him eligible for sainthood.

So Eadmer attached himself to Anselm, learning his life. What is unusual in this case, though, is that Eadmer had the impulse of a true historian. He wanted to write a factual account, so he sought to learn as much as he could about Anselm's earlier years directly from the man himself. Thus Eadmer's *Life of Anselm* is a rare example of an early biography seeking to tell the full story of a man's whole life.

The two men became close friends. Yet something happened to strain their friendship—something that almost caused Eadmer's book to be lost forever. For a long time Anselm did not know that Eadmer was even writing his biography. Yet he gradually became aware that his friend was working on some sort of project. So he

asked Eadmer about this privately. When he saw that Eadmer had
something to hide, Anselm told him either to stop immediately or
else to show him his work.

This request actually came as a relief to Eadmer, who had often
benefited from Anselm's critique of his other writings. At first Anselm
took the same approach with his biography, offering suggestions for
the arrangement of material, clarifying matters of fact, and so forth.
But a few days later Anselm had second thoughts and demanded the
whole book to be destroyed. In all humility, he had to insist that his
life was not worthy to be recorded for posterity.

What was Eadmer to do? He believed his work was important,
but he also wanted to honor the wishes of his friend. Furthermore,
as a monk, it was his duty to obey. In the end, he came up with a
clever solution. He did indeed destroy the original work but not before making a complete copy that he could preserve![1] Thus both of
these good men honored God—Anselm by asking for the biography
to be destroyed, and Eadmer by preserving it.

Anselm's Life

In his biography, Eadmer details many events that are only briefly
mentioned here. Anselm was born to pious parents in 1033 at Aosta
in northern Italy. Anselm's mother prayed often for him, and already
in his teenage years he felt called to the monastic life. For several
years he traveled widely, searching for a spiritual master who could
expand his mind and deepen his devotion to God. At last he came
to the monastery at Bec, in Normandy, where he studied under the
famous teacher Lanfranc. Anselm became a monk of Bec at the age
of twenty-seven.

Anselm's time at Bec was full of scholarly pursuits. There was a
growing library there, and Anselm read widely in the early church
Fathers, especially Augustine. Even as a young scholar, he was drawn
to the contemplation of complex theological problems that required
rigorous analysis. He came to a strong conviction that Holy Scripture

was the truth of God, and that to stand on Scripture was to stand on solid ground. Further, he believed that his calling in life was to study the heart of that truth by exploring the Bible's deepest mysteries.[2] One of his biographers describes the result: Anselm "absorbed the Bible in his thought and language, and allowed his meditations to grow, as a river gathers strength from the springs from which it flows."[3]

The knowledge of God was the love of Anselm's life. To quote one of his most famous sayings, "I long to understand in some degree thy truth, which my heart believes and loves. For I do not seek to understand that I may believe, but I believe in order to understand."[4] To that end, Anselm asked for God's help in his spiritual and intellectual pursuits. "Come then, Lord my God," he prayed, "teach my heart where and how to seek you, where and how to find you."[5] "Teach me to seek you, and reveal yourself to me as I seek, because I can neither seek you if you do not teach me how, nor find you unless you reveal yourself."[6]

At the same time that his mind was seeking understanding, Anselm's heart was growing in godliness. He became devoted to a life of prayer and fasting. As he became more aware of his true spiritual condition, he mourned for his sins. He also became known for the wisdom of his counsel, and other students would seek him out for spiritual advice. For Anselm, the life of a monk was a life of "wholehearted adherence to God in love, together with the faithful among men and women. The closer you come to this the more fully will your will be conformed to the will of God. That can only happen as you empty your heart of all other desires but the desire for God."[7] Anselm wrote in a similar vein to one of the monks at Canterbury: "You have begun to taste that the Lord is sweet. Beware, therefore, that you are not so filled with the savor of the world which flows abundantly over you that you are emptied of the savor of God which flows quickly and secretly away."[8]

In his pursuit of God, Anselm placed a strong emphasis on personal holiness. Once, when he saw a boy teasing a captive bird, he remarked, "That is how the Devil plays with us."[9] Anselm believed that the least sin should be resisted, not just in action but also in thought. One of Anselm's later biographers summarized his approach to the Christian life: he was "a man utterly given up to God, deeply and quietly intent on the contemplation of truths of faith which gave him spiritual, moral, intellectual and aesthetic pleasure all at once."[10]

Early in his time at Bec, Anselm became the head of his monastery; that is to say, he became the abbot. His master, Lanfranc, had been chosen to serve as the Archbishop of Canterbury in England, and Anselm, despite his youth, was the obvious choice to be the successor. He resisted strenuously, wishing that he could pursue his theological studies without the burden of ecclesiastical administration. In the end, though, he accepted the call of God and the unanimous election of the church. In time, he came to embrace his calling as a mentor to younger men in ministry, particularly through his dinner-time conversations. It was customary for most monasteries to hear a theological book read aloud during the evening meal, but, instead, Anselm often gave informal discourses on the virtues of the Christian life or other important topics in theology.

Many years later, when he was sixty (1093), Anselm succeeded Lanfranc again, this time by becoming the Archbishop of Canterbury. At first the great theologian also refused this high honor and heavy administrative responsibility, but in the end the king of England persuaded him to become Anselm of Canterbury.

During his tenure as archbishop, Anselm was caught up in severe conflicts between the kings of England (William II and Henry I) and the popes in Rome (Urban II and Paschal II), each vying for his support and each threatening him for any failure to comply. In the course of one of these conflicts, in which Anselm always tried to serve as a mediator, he was exiled from England and traveled to Rome. There he was regarded as second only to the pope himself, walking just behind him in ecclesiastical processions.

Anselm's Writings

From Rome Anselm traveled to the Italian countryside, where he completed his most famous book: *Cur Deus Homo*, or *Why the God-Man?* In this famous treatise, Anselm developed his doctrine of the atonement, which endures as a lasting achievement in the history of Christian theology. It was characteristic of his doctrine of the atonement that Anselm believed in both the absolute justice and the absolute mercy of God.[11] But this is true of his thought as a whole, as we see from his other writings.

Anselm was prolific, producing many theological treatises on major Christian doctrines. These works bear titles such as *De Incarnatione Verbi* (*On the Incarnation of the Word*), or *De Processione Spiritus Sancti* (*On the Procession of the Holy Spirit*), or *De Conceptu Virginali* (*On the Virgin Birth*). Never one to shy away from difficult problems, in *De Concordia* Anselm also tried to resolve the age-old problem of reconciling human freedom with divine foreknowledge.

Anselm's Proslogion

In philosophy, Anselm's greatest work was the *Proslogion*. The great theologian had become convinced that there must be some way to prove the existence of God to the rational mind—a clear, simple, and indisputable proof for the divine being. Eadmer tells us that for a time Anselm became obsessed with the quest for this proof. He found himself distracted in worship services at the monastery chapel, unable to concentrate on his regular work. Anselm became so preoccupied with his philosophical quest that he began to suspect that the idea of finding an argument for God must be a temptation of the Devil. But still the idea that there must be a proof for God pressed itself in upon his consciousness, until finally the moment came when he grasped his argument with a single act of mental apprehension.

The *Proslogion* is Anselm's attempt to explain this insight to others. Here is how the book begins: "Come, now, little man, come away from your duties a little while, and hide for a space from your tumultuous thoughts. . . . Give yourself up to God and rest for a time in him. Enter the chamber of your mind and shut out everything but God and what helps you to seek him, and with the door closed, seek him out."[12]

Notice that his argument was never intended to function as a sheer exercise of the intellect but out of a sincere desire to know God. It was a spiritual and not merely a philosophical quest. Anselm thus began the *Proslogion* by quoting the fool of Psalm 14, who says in his heart that there is no God. He proceeded to argue that even the fool knows what is meant by God—that when he says that there is no God, he at least knows the definition of who God is. According to this definition, Anselm says, God is "something than which nothing greater can be thought."[13] But by this definition, God must in fact exist. For if God did not exist—if he only existed in the mind, and not in reality—then there would still be something greater that the mind could conceive, namely, a God who really did exist.

At this point, the God that the fool has in mind—namely, a being than which nothing greater can be thought—turns out not to be a being than which something greater *can* be thought after all. The fool's position thus becomes self-contradictory. Anselm concludes that the being "than which nothing greater can be thought" must therefore exist in reality. The existence of God is not simply rational but necessary, the ground of all other thought. Having reached this conclusion, Anselm is moved directly to praise: "And You, Lord our God," he exults, "are this being. You exist so truly, Lord my God, that you cannot even be thought not to exist. And this is as it should be."[14]

Anselm on Prayer

Also worthy of mention are Anselm's extensive pastoral letters and his devout writings on prayer. In fact, during the Middle Ages, the prayers and meditations of Anselm were far more popular than anything else he wrote. These devotional writings are a warm invitation to life with God. "Go apart to be with God for a time," wrote Anselm in one of his letters, "and rest for a while in him."

What was unusual about Anselm's prayers is that they were intended for personal use. Most prayers of the time were liturgical, intended for use in public worship. But Anselm wanted to help believers in their personal relationship with Christ. He wrote not only for his fellow monks but also for educated lay people. His goal was to help people see their sin and need for grace and to express these deep spiritual desires to God in the life of prayer. One scholar comments that whereas in "*Cur Deus Homo* we see the logic of redemption," in Anselm's devotional writings we see "desperate human need and the immeasurable kindness of God."[15]

After two exiles on the Continent, Anselm finally returned to England permanently in 1106. Within a few years, he became seriously ill. He spoke little during his last days on earth but was able to raise his feeble hand to bestow a final blessing on the many friends who came to pay him their final respects. Early on his dying day, a member of the cathedral community read him the gospel for the last time—words of Jesus from Luke about enduring through trials and entering the Father's kingdom, there to eat and to drink at the table of Christ (Luke 22:28–30). The great theologian died in peaceful sleep at the dawn of the breaking day.[16]

Cur Deus Homo

Anselm's lasting theological achievement is his doctrine of the atonement, as explained and defended in *Cur Deus Homo*. In all his writings, Anselm displays a firm confidence in Scripture as the only source of ultimate authority. Within its pages, the Bible contains the authority for every truth that may be discovered. At the same time, Anselm firmly believed in the use of reason. His goal in *Cur Deus Homo* was to develop a doctrine of the atonement based on reason alone. He followed this method because he was writing mainly for the benefit of unbelievers, seeking to answer for them the question, "Why the God-Man?" or "Why did God become a man?"

Cur Deus Homo is divided into two parts. Book One, as Anselm calls it, seeks to show that no one can be saved without the saving work of Jesus Christ in becoming a man and dying on the cross. Book Two seeks to show that human beings were created for eternal happiness, and that this could only be achieved by God becoming a man.

The book's method is to demonstrate these truths in the form of a dialogue with questions and answers. Anselm's conversation partner is one of his fellow monks, a man named Boso. Boso had traveled to Bec in order to get answers to some of his theological questions, much the way skeptics in the 1960s traveled to L'Abri to learn from Francis Schaeffer. Later, when Anselm began working on *Cur Deus Homo*, he summoned Boso to continue their dialogue. Although the book is a literary production rather than the transcript of a conversation, many of the questions that Anselm addresses in *Cur Deus Homo* appear to be questions that Boso actually asked. The two men must have become close friends, because Anselm sent for Boso at the end of his life.

At first Anselm is unsure whether he should answer Boso's questions at all. He fears that his words will not do justice to the mysteries of the gospel, and that therefore readers will end up with a distorted picture of Christ, like one of the ill-conceived paintings of the Savior that Anselm had sometimes seen. But Boso responds with an earnest plea for spiritual help. Style is not important, he says, but only the truth. Please write the gospel truth "for me and for those who with me ask it of you."[17] *Cur Deus Homo* is a book for earnest seekers of spiritual truth. In it, Anselm tries to follow the command of Peter to always be "prepared to make a defense to anyone who asks you for a reason for the hope that is in you" (1 Pet. 3:15).

The first unbelieving objection to the gospel that he considers is the apparent indignity of the incarnation. Why would the very Son of God condescend to enter a woman's womb, to endure childbirth, to suckle at his mother's breast, and then to suffer the difficulties of weariness, hunger, and thirst?[18]

It was all to show his love, Anselm answers. Our surprise at the incarnation of the Son of God shows that we are dealing with a high degree of mercy and grace. Furthermore, there is a certain appropriateness in the way salvation corresponds to sin. What set us wrong in the first place was an act of disobedience by one man; what sets us right is an act of obedience by another man. The fall came from the fruit of a tree; redemption comes by death on a tree. And so forth. These corresponding pictures, as Anselm calls them, point us in the direction of the suitability of Christ and his saving work. Yet he realizes they are not really arguments, so he knows he will have to come up with something more rigorous.

Anselm's next move is to say that God's purpose for the human race needed to stand. He had predetermined to have a people for himself. Now that they had fallen into sin and misery, it was necessary for them somehow to be rescued. But surely, Boso says, this rescue could have been accomplished through another man, a mere man, and yet a man without sin—not a divine Messiah, but a human one.

Yet Anselm saw a difficulty with this means of salvation. If God had created another man without sin to rescue the human race, then we would all owe a debt of undying gratitude to that man. We would be obligated to honor him and not to worship God alone. The only way to avoid this difficulty was for God himself to do the saving.

To show what this saving work required God to do, Anselm explored the fallen condition of lost humanity. He talked about the enslavement of sin, the just anger and righteous wrath of a holy God, and the power of the Devil. Here Anselm clearly distinguished his own view of the atonement from older doctrines. According to the *Christus Victor* theology of the Eastern church, the cross was primarily a victory over the powers of sin, death, and the Devil. According to ransom theories of redemption, the atonement was something owed to Satan. Various theologians picked up on the ransom language of the New Testament and applied it to a Devil's bargain between God and Satan. Some believed that by virtue of sin, the Devil actually had a right to the human race, and that the cross served as a ransom that was paid to the Devil himself. Even Augustine was known to speak of the cross as "the Devil's mousetrap."[19] The cross looked like the defeat of Christ, and thus the Devil was tricked by it, like the bait that leads a mouse into a trap. For in the end the cross turned out to be Satan's defeat, not Satan's victory.

While Anselm recognized that the cross was a ransom, he rejected outright any theology of the atonement that gave too much credit to Satan, believing as he did that the Devil had no legal right to hold people captive. Whatever sinners Satan claimed as his own were stolen from God in the first place, and it could never be right to pay any sort of ransom to a robber and a thief.

Having rejected these inadequate theories of the atonement, Anselm next considered the sufferings of Christ. Some unbelievers would object that it was unjust for Christ to suffer at all. How could it be reasonable for God to offer his own Son up to death—the Son that he loved, a perfect man, who never sinned?[20] If God could not save sinners any other way, then where was his omnipotence? If he could have done it some other way, but didn't, then where was his wisdom?

Anselm answers these objections by emphasizing the voluntary nature of the atonement. The Son was not forced to die but gave himself as the free offering of his own desire. Christ willingly underwent death, steadfastly following the path of obedience unto death as his own cheerful sacrifice.

The Debt of Sin We Owe

To this point, we have not yet come to the main question of Anselm's book, which demonstrates the necessity of the cross and the true doctrine of the atonement. This question deals with sin and its satisfaction, of fully dealing with the problem of sin.

Anselm argued that although man was created for happiness, no one can attain this happiness unless his sins have been forgiven. Yet all of us are guilty of sin. It follows, therefore, that we will never be happy until our sins have been forgiven. This is the conclusion to Anselm's theological syllogism: everyone needs forgiveness.

As Anselm defines it, to sin is to fail to render unto God the obedience we owe. Obedience is our legitimate obligation to God. When we obey, we pay God the honor that he deserves. But when we fail to obey, as we all do, we still owe something to God, for our dishonor to God places us in his debt. "Sinful man," said Anselm, "owes God a debt for sin which he cannot repay." Indeed, at one point Anselm claims that it would be better for the whole universe to perish than for even one glance contrary to the will of God to go unpunished.

Part of Anselm's point of reference for giving honor and repaying debts is the relationship between a servant vassal and his feudal lord. He has often been criticized for seeing the biblical doctrine of sin through the lens of medieval relationships. But it remains the case that God is our Lord, that we owe him honor, and that when we fail to give him the honor that he deserves, we incur a debt of sin. These are all biblical concepts, and Anselm expresses them using biblical language.

One way to see this is simply to substitute the biblical word *glory* for the word *honor*. To say that we ought to honor God is simply to say that he alone deserves the glory. According to Paul, this is the problem with fallen humanity: we do not glorify God. "For although they knew God," the apostle says, "they did not honor him as God or give thanks to him" (Rom. 1:21).

Debt is also a biblical concept. We find it in the Lord's Prayer, among other places. There Jesus gives us this daily petition for confession: "Forgive us our debts" (Matt. 6:12). As far as atonement is concerned, what is important to see is that in order for man to be saved, this debt of sin has to be dealt with. It is not sufficient for us to honor God from this point forward. We cannot simply pay God what we owe him from now on. There must be a restoration of the honor that we have robbed from God. Satisfaction for sin demands a payment of this debt. To anyone who fails to see this, Anselm would reply: "You have not yet considered the exceeding gravity of sin."[21]

Anselm also has a question of his own that he wants to ask Boso, or anyone else who sins: "What will therefore become of you? How can you be saved?"[22] In response, Boso wonders whether it might be possible for God to forgive sin without any satisfaction at all. Could he not simply forgive sin by mercy alone, without exacting any form of payment?

Anselm answers by saying that this would disrupt the moral order of the universe, that it would leave unresolved a dishonor against the nature of God. There must be satisfaction for sin; the symmetry of God's character demands it. If God were simply to dismiss sin, he would no longer be just, and therefore he would no longer be God. Here it should be noted that Anselm was the first theologian to use the language of satisfaction to describe the atoning work of Jesus Christ.

To demonstrate the need for complete satisfaction, Anselm offers an illustration. He imagines a rich man holding a pearl of great price that he is about to place in his treasury. The pearl does not represent the kingdom of God, in this case, but the beauty of one of God's servants, someone destined for the glories of heaven. Suppose that the rich man allows his beautiful pearl to be knocked out of his hand, where it falls into the mud. Would he simply pick up the pearl and put it into his treasury without cleaning it? Instead, would he not do whatever was needed to clean the pearl and restore its true beauty? To become a citizen of heaven, a man must be made sinless by the satisfaction of God.[23]

Yes, Boso says, but if a man is not able to pay God the debt that he owes, shouldn't he be excused? How can it be right for God to demand something which man cannot satisfy? This argument might be reasonable, Anselm responds, if the man had ended up in debt through no fault of his own. But that is hardly the case here. We are in debt because we have indebted ourselves. Here he uses another illustration. Suppose a master tells his servant to carry out a certain task. Suppose further that the master carefully instructs his servant not to throw himself down into a deep hole, from which he cannot escape. Now suppose that the servant proceeds to do exactly what he was told not to do and willfully leaps into a deep pit. Unable to escape, he fails to fulfill his responsibilities to the master. In such a case, should he not be blamed for failing to carry out the task that he was given?[24]

Such is our own unrighteousness. We have failed to do what we ought to do, and we are guilty for it. Though responsible for our sin, we are not able to overcome it. As Anselm puts it, "Sinful man owes God a debt for sin which he cannot repay, and at the same time he cannot be saved without repaying." "This," Boso ruefully admits, "is a very painful conclusion."[25]

The Satisfaction of God

Book Two of *Cur Deus Homo* moves from sin to salvation, showing how God has dealt with the debt that we owe. Anselm begins by returning to an earlier premise, namely, that God has designed us to be happy in our enjoyment of him. Having committed himself to this purpose, he must surely achieve it. Not that God is obligated to save us by any outside necessity, of course, but only by his own gracious and generous commitment to redeem mankind—a voluntary obligation.

To achieve his gracious purpose, God is committed to making satisfaction for sin. Indeed, from what we have already seen, only God is able to do so. Anselm argues that our salvation can be accomplished only if someone pays to God something that is sufficient to make recompense. To be sufficient to make recompense, what is offered to God must be something greater than everything else that exists, apart from God himself. Because God made everything that exists, everything else belongs to him already. Furthermore, the person who makes this payment must be greater than everything that is not God. The only person who satisfies these conditions is God himself. So God must be the one who satisfies the debt of sin.

Satisfaction Made

There is another side to this, however, and with the other side comes another problem. Only God can make satisfaction. But in fact it is really man that ought to make the satisfaction. This is because the debt is man's debt. If God simply paid the debt himself, then man would not be making the satisfaction. Although God could in fact pay for sin, he has not committed any offense. How then can God make satisfaction for man's sin? This seeming dilemma can be resolved only when the debt is paid by someone who is both God and man—one person who is both perfect God and perfect man—the God-man (*Deus homo*).

At this point Boso interrupts to say, "Blessed be God!" Well he should, for here we have one of the high points in the history of theology: a clear statement of the meaning of both the person and the work of Jesus Christ. If we ask, "Why the God-man?" (*Cur Deus homo*), the answer is: because only someone who is both God and man is able to make satisfaction for sin. As man, he is in the right position to make the payment for sin; as God, he has the necessary resources to make the payment for sin. To return to the main question, why did God become man? The answer is that God became a man because this is the only way for us to be saved and thus for God to fulfill his purposes for the human race.

To summarize Anselm's doctrine of the atonement, "we owed a debt we could not pay, while Christ paid a debt he did not owe."[26] Or, to say the same thing in more detail, here is how Boso summarized the climax of Anselm's argument:

> The main point of the question was, why God was made man that by His death He might save mankind, when it would seem that this might have been done in some other way: in answer to which

you showed by many and necessary proofs that the restoration of human nature neither ought to have been left undone: nor could have been, unless man should repay what for sin he owed unto God: which was so heavy a debt that as no one unless he were man, ought, so unless he were God, he could not, pay it; and therefore that some one must be man who also is God. Wherefore it was needful that God should assume humanity in unity of person, so that the nature which ought to pay, and could not have paid, should be in person One who could.[27]

The Nature of the Incarnation

Having come to a firm conclusion on the doctrine of the atonement, Anselm reflects further on the nature of the incarnation, to consider how it is that the divine nature and the human nature can be united in one person. This is one of the great strengths of Anselm's work, his lasting achievement: in *Cur Deus Homo* he brings the doctrines of incarnation and atonement into their proper relationship, showing the necessity of both natures of Christ for his saving work on the cross.

In keeping with the Council of Chalcedon, Anselm argues that the divine nature and the human nature of Christ must be kept distinct, not mixed together or confused with one another. Yet they must be joined together in one person. The divine is not obliged to make satisfaction; the human is not able to make satisfaction. But when they are joined in one person, these two natures make full satisfaction for sin.

This person—both fully human and fully divine, the God-man—must of necessity be born to the human race. He could not be a fresh creation but must come directly from Adam so as to belong to humanity's fallen race. This is in keeping with the teaching of Scripture: "When the fullness of time had come, God sent forth his Son, born of woman" (Gal. 4:4). Or again, "Since therefore the children share in flesh and blood, he himself likewise partook of the same things. . . . He had to be made like his brothers in every respect, . . . to make propitiation for the sins of the people" (Heb. 2:14, 17).

Jesus made this propitiation by offering his precious blood to God in the infinite worth of his divine nature. According to Anselm, what the God-man gave to make satisfaction for sin needed to be more valuable than our sin is detestable. And so it was, for the life of the Son of God is perfectly meritorious and infinitely precious.

Anselm's Influence

To summarize everything we have said thus far, here is how the famous church historian Jaroslav Pelikan assessed Anselm's doctrine of the atonement:

> Christ was "the God-man," who was not under the necessity of dying (since he was almighty) nor under the obligation of dying (since he was sinless), but who of his own free will had assumed human nature into the person of the Son of God, so that by his dying he might voluntarily achieve the satisfaction owed by humanity and make it available to his fellowmen (since he did not need it for himself).[28]

This doctrine of the atonement did not meet with full acceptance in Anselm's own time. The most strenuous objections came from Peter Abelard, who argued that the value of the work of Christ was primarily as an example of the way that human life ought to be lived. The death of Christ was not satisfactory, in the sense of providing atonement for sin, but exemplary, in the sense of showing the way to suffer and die with courage. Similar notions are still with us. Whenever we hear Jesus presented more as an example than as a Savior, we are hearing the sons and daughters of Abelard.

Yet theologically orthodox Christians have accepted the main outlines of Anselm's ever since. His was the definitive doctrine of the atonement, and thus it had a dominant influence on many late medieval theologians. We often hear echoes of his theology of satisfaction in their writings on soteriology. We find it, for example, in Dante, who said, "If there had not been a satisfaction for sin through the death of Christ, we would still be 'by nature children of wrath.'" We find it in Ubertino of Casale, who said, "No one could render satisfaction for the whole human race except God, and no one owed it to God except man." We find it in John Hus, the famous disciple of John Wycliffe, who said that "no one can render satisfaction for himself, except through the principal satisfaction made by the Lord Jesus Christ."

We also find Anselm's doctrine in Thomas à Kempis, who is more commonly known for his devotional writings. But as far as his theology was concerned, Thomas believed that by Christ's death on the cross he "redeemed us and rendered satisfaction to God the Father for our sins." We find the same theology in Gabriel Biel, who taught that when mankind "was not able to satisfy the divine justice, the Father of mercies gave his Son, who assumed a human nature, innocent and pure, and by offering to justice rendered satisfaction." And God accepted "this sacrifice of Christ, namely, his death, as a satisfaction for sin."[29]

Anselm also exercised a decisive influence on the Reformers, who took his doctrine of the atonement and improved upon it. This is especially true of John Calvin, who followed Anselm in describing the doctrine of the atonement in judicial terms. Like Anselm, Calvin used judicial categories such as the payment of a debt, the rescue from a criminal sentence by a substitute, and the declaration of justification to describe the atoning work of Jesus Christ.[30] He also used Anselm's familiar language of satisfaction: "Our Lord came forth as true man . . . to present our flesh as the price of satisfaction to God's righteous judgment."[31] Or again, "by the sacrifice of his death [Jesus] blotted out our own guilt and made satisfaction for our sins."[32]

Calvin also added new dimensions to Anselm's formulation. He made it clear that Christ's sacrifice was not simply a gift of infinite value that honored God and merited his favor, but that in his death

Christ actually suffered the punishment that we deserve for our sins. In other words, Calvin presented the doctrine of penal substitution, the payment of sin by a vicarious death, suffered on our behalf.

For Anselm, the choice was either for our sins to be punished or for Christ to satisfy God with an infinitely valuable sacrifice. For Calvin, the choice was either for us to suffer the punishment for our own sins or for Christ to suffer that punishment for us on the cross. Calvin understood more clearly than Anselm that the debt of sin makes us liable to the wrath of God, and that therefore the satisfaction Jesus gives is not simply by honoring God, but even more by suffering his wrath on our behalf.[33]

There are other aspects of the atonement that Calvin clarified as well. He emphasized the active obedience of Christ. It is not just the suffering death of Jesus that saves us but also his sinless life. Anselm believed that Jesus lived a perfect life, of course, but this was only important because it meant that death was not something Jesus owed to God, so that when he died, his death could count for us. But Calvin believed that "the whole life of Christ"—"the whole course of his obedience"—was necessary for our salvation. Jesus had to fulfill the law's demand for our obedience, not just suffer the penalty for our disobedience. Only then could his active righteousness become our own. We need both his substitute perfection and his substitute punishment. Here Calvin presented his doctrine of union with Christ, which is also absent from Anselm. According to Calvin, we are joined to Jesus Christ, and in this union, our unrighteousness is imputed to Christ, and his righteousness is imputed to us. We are reconciled to God by a blessed exchange.[34]

Unfortunately, although it has long been regarded as Christian orthodoxy, Anselm's doctrine of the atonement has come under renewed attack in recent years. Indeed, that is one of the main reasons why this book is necessary. Anselm's doctrine may not be the final word, but what he learned from the Scriptures and taught to the church remains of lasting importance for Christian theology.

As modern theologians advocate a new doctrine of the atonement, their frustration with Anselm is evident. One English theologian who says that those "who revel in ideas such as that Christ was made a sacrifice to appease an angry God, or that the cross was a legal transaction in which an innocent victim was made to pay the penalty for the crimes of others, a propitiation of a stern God, find no support in Paul. These notions came into Christian theology by way of the legalistic minds of the medieval churchmen; they are not biblical Christianity."[35]

Similarly, John Caputo says we need to move beyond "a God who forgives us only if the divine sense of honor or justice, offended by sin, is satisfied by the violence of the crucifixion." We need to start with the New Testament, he says, "not from entrenched theological traditions that go back to Anselm."[36] C. F. D. Moule went so far as to say that when reading Anselm or his followers, one has "difficulty recognizing the good news of the gospel."[37]

Yet when such theologians start to list the medieval ideas that we supposedly need to outgrow, they include the following:

- "Sin is primarily law-breaking, and God judges sin with death."
- "Sin separates us from God, creating a great chasm of broken fellowship."
- "God cannot look on sin or overlook it or simply forgive it. For God's wrath to be satisfied, it must be punished."
- "Jesus bore the wrath of God on the Cross in my place to bridge the gulf between sinful man and holy God."[38]

It seems obvious from this list that the real quibble these theologians have is not with Anselm but with the Bible itself. Yet we are told that these doctrinal truths are medieval, not biblical, and that therefore they should not determine our doctrine of the atonement.

Anselm's Great Contribution

In truth, Anselm had a much clearer idea about what the Bible teaches about sin and salvation, and about the incarnation and the atonement, than many contemporary theologians. His great contribution was to offer an account of Christ's satisfaction for sin. As the perfect man, Christ fully identifies with our humanity and bears the burden of our sin. As perfect God, Christ's death is of infinite value in making satisfaction for the guilt of all our sin. This was Anselm's basic thesis: that only a God-man can make the satisfaction by which man can be saved. Here is how Anselm later summarized his own doctrine of the atonement:

> Unchanging truth and clear reason demand that the sinner give to God, in place of the honor stolen, something greater. . . . But human nature by itself did not have this payment. And without the required satisfaction human nature could not be reconciled, lest Divine Justice leave a sin unreckoned-with in His kingdom. Therefore, Divine Goodness gave assistance. The Son of God assumed a human nature into His own person, so that in this person He was the God-man, who possessed what exceeded . . . every debt which sinners ought to pay. And since He owed nothing for Himself, He paid this sum for others who did not have what they were indebted to pay.[39]

The way for us to respond to this gift of grace is by faith. *Cur Deus Homo* is sometimes criticized for saying too little about personal trust in Jesus Christ. Yet Anselm says almost everything about faith that needs to be said. He turns people away from thinking that there is anything sinners themselves can do to satisfy God. He has the Father offer salvation as a free gift to anyone who will receive his Son. He presents faith as the only way for anyone to receive the merit of Christ's death on the cross. And after answering many questions that unbelief is bound to raise, Anselm at last turns to his friend Boso and says:

You should require this at their hands in whose name you speak (who do not believe Christ to be needful to man's salvation): let them say how man can be saved without Christ. Which if they can in nowise prove, let them cease from ridiculing us, come over and join themselves to us who doubt not but that man can be saved by Christ, or let them despair of this being in any way possible. From which, if they shrink, let them with us believe in Christ, that they may be saved.[40]

Yes, let us believe in Christ so that we may be saved. Then, as we consider the wonder of the incarnation and the atonement, we may stand before the God of all grace and say what Boso said, once he understood Anselm's famous doctrine of the atonement: "Nothing more reasonable, delightful, desirable, could the world hear. Therefore I hence conceive so great confidence that I can hardly express the greatness of my heart's exultant joy."[41]

THE REFORMATION CONSENSUS ON THE ATONEMENT

W. Robert Godfrey

When it comes to considering the doctrines of the Protestant Reformation, the best place to start is with Martin Luther's Ninety-five Theses. Luther, of course, was the great pioneer of the Reformation, and it was the posting of the Ninety-five Theses on October 31, 1517, that is usually seen as the formal beginning of the Reformation. That date marks the moment at which Luther began to move from being an obscure monk teaching at a small university of not much prominence to the path that he trod to becoming one of the most famous people of the sixteenth century.

The Ninety-five Theses: Not a Protestant Document

Nonetheless, there is considerable irony to the fact that we look back to the Ninety-five Theses as the beginning moment of the Reformation, for the Ninety-five Theses are not at all a Protestant document. Those of you who have read them will know that the Ninety-five Theses still breathe the spirit of medieval Roman Catholicism. Indeed, one of the things Luther says in the Ninety-five Theses is that if anyone denies the apostolic character of the indulgences, let him be an anathema. Luther wrote the Ninety-five Theses not to attack indulgences but to attack the abuse of them. In actuality, we can read the Ninety-five Theses to get a good sense for late medieval Roman Catholic theology at its best.

In the very first thesis, Luther makes his basic point by stating that when our Lord and Master Jesus Christ said repent, he called for the entire life of believers to be one of penitence. How are Christians to live? Not just by occasionally buying an indulgence or going to the sacrament of penance and confessing their sins to a priest and being absolved; their whole life is to be characterized by repentance, that is, by sorrow for their sin.

That is not a bad statement in and of itself, but it is very much in the spirit of late medieval Christianity, which constantly taught the need to be more serious and to work harder. It is not enough to be occasionally penitent; one must be constantly penitent. This emphasis becomes even more obvious toward the end of Luther's theses. Thesis 92 cries out, "Away then with those prophets who say to Christ's people, peace, peace, where there is no peace." Luther is quoting Jeremiah 6:14, where the prophet pronounces woe on the false prophets, for "they have healed the wound of my people lightly, saying, 'Peace, peace,' when there is no peace." Luther was saying, in the spirit of Jeremiah, that indulgence sellers such as John Tetzel were healing the wounds of God's people lightly, promising peace when there was no peace.

Luther is critiquing a message of cheap grace, one that advocates merely buying an indulgence, a plenary indulgence that covers all sins: past, present, and future. The message is this: "Pay your money, and you're safe. When you get to the gates of heaven, just show Peter the indulgence, and you'll pass right through."

Luther critiques this as saying "peace, peace" where there is no peace. So in Thesis 93, he writes, "Hail, hail to all those prophets who say to Christ's people, the cross, the cross where there is no cross." Luther is warning people that merely talking about the cross is insufficient; one must actually take up the cross. To make this perfectly clear, he said in Thesis 94, "Christians should be exhorted to be zealous to follow Christ their head through penalties, deaths, and hells."

We can immediately observe that there is not much emphasis on grace or faith in the Ninety-five Theses. There is nothing of Luther's later trademark teaching on justification. There is no real gospel. Luther is saying that the Christian must take up the cross and live a self-denying life. That is a better way of hoping to get to heaven than buying an indulgence.

The theology of the Ninety-five Theses is not Protestantism. Rather, it is the best of late medieval Roman Catholicism. This reminds us that there are all sorts of ways of talking about the cross while not really getting the cross right.

Medieval Theology

Anselm, Thomas Aquinas, and others could write rather eloquently about the absolute necessity and the foundational character of the cross of Christ. Christ on the cross is the meritorious cause of salvation, insisted medieval Roman Catholics over and over again. So where did they go wrong?

The best way to understand what happened in medieval theology is to see that while the cross of Christ remained foundational in many ways, the cross of Christ was not central in the message preached to the people. Conveyed to them was the idea that Christ on the cross made salvation possible, but people still have a responsibility to connect with that Christ so that Christ's merit could become theirs. The center of medieval religion then became that work to acquire the merit of Christ. That process involved, on the one hand, the work of priests on behalf of the people and, on the other hand, the work of Christians on their own behalf.

To a certain extent, it seemed that the cross remained central in the medieval church. During the late Middle Ages it was common to see a cross on top of a Roman Catholic church. Crosses decorated the interior of such churches too, including the altar. From a visual perspective, the cross seemed central. But in reality the cross receded behind the more central work of priests and of Christians.

The Roman Church Today

The medieval Roman Catholic Church was much the same as the Roman Catholic Church today, where we still find a priest wearing priestly garments performing priestly activities around an altar. That priestly activity of the altar culminates in a sacrifice.

There has been some discussion of late about Question 80 of the Heidelberg Catechism, which concludes, "Thus the Roman mass is nothing essentially than a denial of the once for all sacrifice of Jesus Christ in a cursed idolatry." Some are saying that this does not accurately represent the Roman Catholic position. But the Heidelberg Catechism, historically, in light of what we believe the Bible teaches, is exactly right. The Roman Catholic Church believes that the priest stands at the altar to offer a propitiatory sacrifice of Jesus Christ, turning away the wrath of God. Rome officially teaches, both from the Council of Trent and in its latest Catholic Catechism, that the mass is a propitiatory sacrifice.

Rome says that the mass is not a new sacrifice; it is actually the sacrifice of Jesus Christ on the cross. It is hard to see, however, how what goes on at the altar is a propitiatory sacrifice without taking away from the fullness and finality of the propitiation of Christ on the cross two thousand years ago. Consider the teaching of Hebrews 9:24–28:

> For Christ has entered, not into holy places made with hands, which are copies of the true things, but into heaven itself, now to appear in the presence of God on our behalf. Nor was it to offer himself repeatedly, as the high priest enters the holy places every year with blood not his own, for then he would have had to suffer repeatedly since the foundation of the world. But as it is, he has

appeared once for all at the end of the ages to put away sin by the sacrifice of himself. And just as it is appointed for man to die once, and after that comes judgment, so Christ, having been offered once to bear the sins of many, will appear a second time, not to deal with sin but to save those who are eagerly waiting for him.

Notice the comparison that Hebrews is drawing between the death of a human being and the sacrifice of Christ. The death of a human being happens only once. It is unrepeatable. It cannot be continued. Once it happens, it is over. That is the character of the death of Christ, the sacrifice of Christ. It happened once—once for all—and then it was over.

> And every priest stands daily at his service, offering repeatedly the same sacrifices, which can never take away sins. But when Christ had offered for all time a single sacrifice for sins, he sat down at the right hand of God, waiting from that time until his enemies should be made a footstool for his feet. For by a single offering he has perfected for all time those who are being sanctified. . . . Where there is forgiveness of these [that is, sins], there is no longer any offering for sin. (Heb. 10:11–14, 18)

Once forgiveness is accomplished on the cross of Christ, there is no longer any offering for sin. The medieval church had fundamentally lost its way on this issue, and the Reformation was part of what began to restore the biblical religion.

Part of the tragedy of the medieval church was that it basically restored Old Testament institutions of priest and altar and sacrifice, which were meant to be preparation for our understanding the work of Christ. If there never had been an Old Testament priesthood, how would we have understood that Jesus was our great high priest? If there had never been an Old Testament sacrificial system, how would we have understood John the Baptist when he said, "Behold, the Lamb of God, who takes away the sin of the world" (John 1:29)? If there had never been an Old Testament altar, how would we have understood the character of the cross?

Those Old Testament institutions of priesthood, sacrifice, and altar were indispensable to prepare the hearts and minds of God's people to understand all that God was going to do in Jesus Christ for our salvation. But after Christ fulfilled the priesthood, the sacrifice, and the altar, reinstituting them distracts from Christ. Thus, the mass leads us away from Christ, obscuring the fullness and the finality of his atoning work.

That is the tragedy of the Roman Church—its emphasis on a priesthood that it still sees as propitiatory. So our differences with Rome on these points are not minor. They go to the very heart of the centrality of the cross and the question as to whether Christ, once for all, sacrificed himself for sin, ascended into heaven, and sits at the right hand of the Father as a priest no longer suffering for us but still interceding for us and awaiting the day when he will return in glory and make all things new. Rome's theology cannot really be squared with what's being said in Hebrews 9 and 10, and that is what the Reformation began to recover.

The New Babylonian Captivity

As Martin Luther began to think through the implications of centering Christianity in the work of priests, he did not do so as a rebel. He talked about how, at his first mass, he almost couldn't carry out his work as priest. It was so emotionally intense for him because he believed that, as a newly ordained priest, he was performing a miracle. He believed that when he uttered the words of consecration, the bread in his hands ceased to be bread and became exclusively and entirely the body of Jesus Christ. The priest was called upon after the consecration to hold up the bread, and Luther said his hand shook so much that he could hardly do it. He believed he was holding Jesus Christ in his hands.

What were the people to do? The altar boys rang the bells, and everyone was to kneel and worship because there, in the bread, was Jesus Christ. Roman Catholics do not believe such worship is idolatry, because what they are worshiping is not bread anymore; it's Jesus Christ. When they kneel and worship, they worship Christ.

But we, as Protestants, believe that the Bible doesn't say that bread turns fully and entirely into the body of Jesus Christ. Therefore, when a priest holds up bread, Protestants believe that bowing down and worshiping it is idolatry. To do so is to worship bread.

In 1520, a little less than three years after the posting of the Ninety-five Theses, Luther wrote a treatise called "The Babylonian Captivity of the Church," in which he reflected on the sacraments. He said the greatest error of Rome pertained to its belief in a eucharistic sacrifice, because it takes the attention away from Christ and his cross and puts the attention on the work of priests. Luther condemned this as both unbiblical and pastorally harmful.

The medieval church had taught that the way that grace flows in to the believer is by use of the sacraments and by trying to live in love, believing what the church teaches. The great aim of the believer, according to the medieval church, is to acquire enough grace to be acceptable in the sight of God. Since God loves only the lovable, the whole duty and purpose of the believer's life is to try to become more lovable, which is done by acquiring grace through the sacraments, through a life of self-sacrifice, penitence, and suffering, and through a life of love toward others. The great hope is that, at the time of death, the believer's grace quotient will be sufficient for lovability and, therefore, acceptable to God. This approach to Christianity is a rocky road, because any time a believer commits a mortal sin (that is, a deadly sin) he or she loses all grace and has to start over at ground zero. Therefore, it is not possible for any Christian to know in this life that he or she is saved.

During my seminary days, I went to chapel one day to hear a Protestant minister who was just back from Rome, where he had met with Pope Paul VI. He told us, "I think the pope is about to become a Protestant." Well, we all perked up our ears. He explained, "I spoke to the pope about salvation and found that he has no assurance of it." But of course, the pope doesn't have any assurance of salvation! That's part of his theology. Popes, no more than anyone else, can be assured of their salvation. Popes have to struggle just as hard to live and die in the state of grace as anybody else. The lack of assurance inherent to Roman Catholic theology is just as true today as it was in Luther's time, and it is just as true for popes as for paupers.

Luther's Protestant Theology

After 1517 Luther began to realize that the Bible does not stress our working or the priests' working. It seems to be all about Jesus' working. In 1518, only a few months after the posting of the Ninety-five Theses, Luther went to give some lectures at Heidelberg. There, he delivered what came to be known as the Heidelberg Disputation. This is where Luther's Protestant theology was clearly articulated for the first time.

He said there are two kinds of theologies we have to choose between. One is a theology of glory, in which salvation is by human effort, man's cooperation with grace. The focus in the theology of glory is all on the individual. The second kind is the theology of the cross, in which salvation is based solely on Christ's work as he hung on the cross, the most unexpected place we could ever think God would be. Surely, people think, God would be more glorified by performing some grand gesture. But Luther insisted that God took our sin on himself—our sin, our burden, our weakness and failure—and bore it on the cross, which surprises us.

That is part of the problem, even for believers: we have been Christians for so long that the surprise goes out of it. Jesus on the cross? "Well, of course," we say. Instead, our reaction should be, "Jesus on the cross—how can that be? Jesus, the sinless Son of God, the eternal second person of the Trinity, on the cross? Jesus abandoned and dying on the cross? How is that possible?" Yet that's where God does his work. That is where all the work for our salvation has been done.

Luther began to see that we cannot add to that work. Jesus says, "I must do for you what you cannot do for yourself. You cannot help me out. You cannot add just a little bit." There are some works to which any addition is a subtraction. By trying, we only take away from it; we mar and diminish it. That's what Luther finally understood. What the church had told him would never work, for the glory of salvation is that Christ has done everything for us. What he asks of us is to believe him, to trust him, and to rely on him.

That is why the Reformation was so insistent about the contrast between faith and faithfulness, between faith and love, between faith and works. The contrast is not that Protestants don't believe in faithfulness or don't believe in love or good works. They do, but they believe the place of love and works is in the life of the justified Christian after he or she has been justified. For justification, however, we have to look away from ourselves, which is what faith is all about. Faith is to look away from ourselves to Christ and to rest in him, to trust and rely on him. That is what Luther taught with such amazing clarity.

Luther was a sweet preacher of grace. He could be ferocious at times with those who didn't get it, but he longed for people to sense how God had drawn near to them in love through the cross of Jesus Christ. In one of his sermons, Luther wrote that the first thing you see in Christ is that he does not look at anyone with a sour face. I see a lot of Christians with sour faces; at least, that is the impression we get with a lot of people. Nor, said Luther, does Jesus treat anyone in an unfriendly manner or threaten and drive anyone away from himself. He invites and draws all men in the kindliest manner, both with his words and with his bearing.

It is true that Jesus was hard on some of the Pharisees because he saw the hardness of their hearts. Jesus saw their opposition and, like Luther, he challenged them to repent and believe. But Luther's point is essentially true. He asserted:

> [Jesus] shows himself as a servant who wants to help everybody. Furthermore, he lets himself be crucified for you and freely sheds his blood. All this you see with your eyes and with your ears you hear, nothing but friendly, sweet, and comforting words such as "Let not your heart be troubled. Come to Me all who labor and are heavy laden. Whoever believes in Me shall not be lost, but have eternal life." The Gospel of John is full of such verses.

Luther stresses all of this so that we would realize that we don't have to get ready to come to Jesus. We don't have to change our moral character and improve it vastly to come to Jesus. We don't have to put on our best coat and tie to come to Jesus. We are invited to come just as we are, Luther says. We are to come recognizing that the only thing we have to give Jesus is our sin. It is the only thing we can offer him. It is the only work you can do for him. If you are a sinner, you are ready, and he welcomes you. In this reformation of the doctrine of justification, Luther restored the very emphasis that we find in the New Testament.

John Calvin's Contribution

John Calvin taught about the work of Christ and the atonement in ways very similar to Luther. What a tragic injustice that John Calvin is presented as some kind of legalist with a sour face! I have written a little book on Calvin, *John Calvin: Pilgrim and Pastor*. I gave it that title because Calvin made his own spiritual pilgrimage, coming to understand the gospel and then becoming a fervent preacher of that gospel. Calvin did all his work as a theologian and a biblical commentator for the purpose of becoming a better pastor and helping others to be better Christians.

The heart of Calvin can be seen in just a few passages from a sermon that Calvin preached on Ephesians 1:7:

> But let us notice here how St. Paul uses two words to express how we were reconciled to God. First he sets down the ransom or redemption which amounts to the same thing, and afterward he sets down the forgiveness of sins. How then does it come about that God's wrath is pacified and we are made at one with him and that he even accepts and acknowledges us as His children. It is by pardoning our sins, says St. Paul, and furthermore, because pardon necessitates redemption. He yolks the two together. The truth is that in respect to us, God blotted out our sins of His own free goodness and shows Himself altogether bountiful and does not look for any payment for it at our hands. . . . In fact what man is able to make satisfaction for the least fault that he has committed?[1]

God is bountiful, John Calvin says. Do you believe that? God is bountiful. A little later Calvin writes:

> But for all this, the atonement which is freely bestowed in respect of us costs the Son of God very dear. For He found no other payment than the shedding of His own blood so that He made Himself our surety both in body and soul and answered for us before God's judgment to win an absolution for us. Our Lord Jesus Christ, I say, entered into the work both body and soul, for it would not have been enough for Him to have suffered so cruel and ignominious a death in the sight of men, but it was necessary for Him also to bear such horrible anguish in Himself as if God had become His judge, for He gave Himself up on behalf of sinners to make full satisfaction. . . . So you see why St. Paul had joined together the word redemption.[2]

Then Calvin stresses how utterly dependent we are upon God:

> Therefore whenever we intend to seek God's favor and mercy, let us fasten the whole of our minds on the death and passion of our Lord Jesus Christ that we may there find a means by which

to appease God's wrath. . . . Furthermore, seeing that our sins are
done away by such payment and satisfaction let us understand that
we cannot bring anything of our own by which to be reconciled
to God, and in this, we see how the devil has by his craft cut off
all hope of salvation from the world by causing it to be believed
that every man must ransom himself and make his own atonement
with God.[3]

Calvin insists that our refuge must be in Christ. The sacrifice of his
death serves to purchase an everlasting atonement for us, so that we
must always flee to it for refuge. If you have been to Saint Peter's
Cathedral in Geneva, where Calvin preached, you know it is a big
church and seats a lot of people. People in Calvin's day were required
to come to church. They got fined if they didn't. And a lot of them
weren't happy to be there. Calvin was not preaching to a friendly,
sympathetic crowd all of the time.

On a good day, he would write in letters to his friends that he
didn't know if in Geneva there were ten converted people in a hundred. On a bad day, he would write that even one in a hundred didn't
seem likely. He was preaching to a lot of people whom he suspected
were not genuinely reconciled to God. So what did he preach to them?
He pointed them to Christ and his atoning blood, to the place we
must always flee for refuge—the sacrifice of Jesus Christ.

Calvin wrote, "Although then Christ is in a general view redeemer
of the world, yet His death and passion are of no advantage to any but
such as receive that which St. Paul shows us here. So we see that when
we once know the benefits brought to us by Christ, and which He daily
offers us by His Gospel, we must also be joined to Him by faith."[4]
Hearing about what Christ has done is not enough; it is not enough
to know. One has to believe. One must trust. That is what Calvin
preached. He was, like Luther, a sweet preacher of the gospel.

The ringing cries of the Reformation were *Christ alone*, *grace
alone*, and *faith alone*. These weren't mere slogans, clever sayings that
today we can put on bumper stickers. These cries expressed an effort

to understand the very heart and mind of God for the redemption of our souls. Christ's work alone, not our work; Christ's grace alone, not our cooperation; faith in Christ alone, not our loving. That is how we become right with God. That is our hope. And that is the power of Christian living.

Lutherans and Calvinists

While it is correct to stress the shared approach of Lutherans and Calvinists to the doctrine of the atonement, we should note that there are some different emphases. One of these differences involves the role of the law in a Christian's life. Much has been written about the contrast, but I want to suggest that both Calvinists and Lutherans are agreed that the real impetus and motivation to holiness is the gospel. Both are agreed that the law helps us know what holiness looks like. The law makes clear to us what is pleasing to our heavenly Father. The law is indispensable and invaluable. But in the deepest sense our desire to be holy doesn't come from a fear engendered by the law. Our desire to be holy is enjoined by the love of Jesus Christ for us. If we have been loved with such a great love, how can it not inflame love for him in our hearts?

Of course, the law plays a role that is absolutely necessary. But the motive that drives us to pursue holiness is a love for God that springs from the gospel, from the fact that God loves us. The Reformation makes this point about the centrality of the gospel wonderfully and beautifully clear. Reformed Puritans, for example, were very serious about trying to live a holy life because they were so gripped by the glory of Christ's redeeming work for them.

Real gospel preaching never leads to lawlessness and indifference. It is not possible to be truly engaged with Jesus Christ as the Savior of your soul and be indifferent to how you live with him. The Puritans gave themselves to the careful study of Scripture, asking over and over how they could please God more. They sought to please God not in order to get right with God, but because they were right with God.

Differences between Lutherans and Calvinists

There are, however, points where Lutherans and Calvinists ultimately differ. One of these points is not a true difference but, rather, an error into which some Calvinists have fallen—a reluctance to affirm Christ's free offer of the gospel to all.

The Offer of the Gospel to All

Luther's passion for the gospel led him to say that in a profound sense Christ loves every person. Only those who will not come will be lost. Luther saw a fullness in the redemption of Jesus Christ so that we can say Christ died for all. As the Reformed thought more about this issue, they shared a number of Luther's concerns. Calvin, for example, preached passionately, calling all who heard him to come to faith. Some Calvinists have felt restrained in giving a gospel invitation to everyone, but they are at odds with the practice of Calvin himself.

Some believe the gospel invitation, "Christ died for you," goes out indiscriminately to all, but the Scriptures never say that, of course. Calvin and the Reformed realize that the fullness of gospel preaching requires us to say to everyone who hears us, "Come, and in coming you will be saved. In coming you'll know that Jesus died for you. In coming you'll be redeemed." This is what the apostles regularly did; they preached belief and repentance. Everyone who heard was invited to come and believe. Likewise, the prophet Ezekiel cried out with great compassion, "As I live, declares the Lord God, I have no pleasure in the death of the wicked, but that the wicked turn from his way and live; turn back, turn back from your evil ways, for why will you die, O house of Israel?"(Ezek. 33:11).

This is not Arminian preaching. This is prophetic and apostolic preaching. If you can't preach like that, you are not a real Calvinist. More importantly, you are not following the apostolic example. Of course, we know that no one can come unless the Spirit draws him (John 6:44). We know sinners can believe only as a gift of the Holy Spirit. But the work of a preacher is to try to be a vehicle that the Spirit can use at his pleasure. Such a vehicle is the preacher who says, "Come, come now, and in coming there's a fullness and perfection of redemption for you."

Our job is to preach to the worst of sinners and plead with them to come. Yet over time a kind of Reformed Christianity developed where all a preacher could say to the unconverted is, "Wait, maybe grace will zap you." But no apostle ever told sinners to wait, and neither did Calvin.

The Extent of the Atonement

There is another matter on which Lutherans and Calvinists have disagreed, not merely by accident but sincerely and thoughtfully. This is the matter of the extent of the atonement. The question is, "For whom did Jesus substitute himself, and for whom did he offer a sacrifice of atonement?" Calvinists have asserted that if Christ was a substitute, a sacrifice, and a satisfaction for all people and every individual, then surely that must mean all people and every individual will be saved. If everyone has a substitute, a sacrifice, and a satisfaction, then mustn't they be saved?

When I was in college, an evangelical friend was trying to witness to an unbeliever, and he told the unbeliever, "God loves you." The unbeliever replied, "That's great to know. I guess I'm safe." The evangelical didn't know what to do. If God loves you, then you must be safe. The Calvinists have thought very carefully about this. For whom was Christ a substitute? For whom was he a satisfaction? For whom was he a sacrifice? The Reformed say that Christ was those things for the elect, that is, for those whom God in all eternity had planned to save.

It is interesting that Luther believed in election, but he never saw that implication of it. If the Father has elected some to life from eternity, and if the Spirit takes the benefits of Christ and applies them to the elect, in time, to bring them to faith, then surely it must be that Christ died on the cross for the elect with the intention of saving them. That is not just a logical conclusion, but it is the explicitly stated conclusion of Scripture. Hebrews 9:28, to give just one of many examples, says, "So Christ, having been offered once to bear the sins of many." Not the sins of all, but of many—that is, the elect.

Reformed theology has made a helpful distinction between the *sufficiency* of the death of Christ and the *efficiency* of the death of Christ. What is the sufficiency of the death of Christ? Or, to put it another way, if God had elected more people, would Christ have had to suffer more? If God had elected fewer people, would Christ have had to suffer less? No, we reply, for the sufficiency of the suffering of the death of Christ is of infinite value. It was enough, as the Reformed theologians loved to say, to save the whole world and a thousand worlds besides. That is the value—the infinite value and sufficiency—of the death of Christ.

But the death of Christ is also efficient. It is effective. It accomplishes its purpose. Its intention is for the elect alone. Therefore, Christ is a substitute, a sacrifice, and a satisfaction for his own people. As the angel told Mary's betrothed, Joseph, the virgin-born baby should be named Jesus, "for he will save *his people* from their sins" (Matt. 1:21).

Some people today, especially when they hear the word *elect*, think that this must refer to just a tiny, narrow little group. Perhaps this is because Reformed Christians tend to feel that there are so few of us. But notice what the Scripture says: Christ bore the sins of "many" (Heb. 9:28). Christ will have a great people on the last day.

There will be many gathered to glory. He is making a new heaven and a new earth in which the many redeemed in Christ will dwell.

B. B. Warfield used to say that there will be more in heaven than in hell. That may have been a bit optimistic. But we should not have a little, narrow view, as if the elect were just a handful, or as an old friend of mine used to say, "just the select of the elect." Scripture says it is a great multitude that cannot be numbered.

What a glory this is to the saving work of our Lord Jesus Christ! He did not die for a little group. So when we hear about the work of the Spirit in Korea and Africa today, we should not be so uncertain as to what it all means and how many could be true believers. The Spirit is at work, holding up the gospel of Christ, and there are many coming in. What a glorious thing it is that they are coming because the Father from all eternity chose them. They are coming because the Son hung on the cross and thought of them. And they are coming because the Holy Spirit is working in the hearts of those elect to gather them.

That is what we believe as Reformed Christians. It is one of the ways we say, "Glory to God alone. It's all to him. It's all from him. It's all of him." It is a consistent way of saying it is not our wisdom or our goodness or our accomplishment, but it is the work of our God. It is not a way of limiting the love of Christ or the work of Christ. It is, rather, a way of showing how utterly complete and full and sufficient and effective Christ's atoning work is.

Bold Shall I Stand

On the eve of the Protestant Reformation, as Martin Luther prepared to nail his Ninety-five Theses to the Wittenberg castle church door, the great masses of Christendom were being taught to look for salvation from the priests and from their own good works. Perhaps the best way to understand the difference made by Luther's recovery of the gospel of grace, and the Reformation consensus on the atoning work of Jesus Christ, is to listen to the hymnody that resulted. It is not by chance that the heart of the Reformation is passed on to us in its hymnody.

There may be no single hymn that better captures the cross-centered spirit of the Reformation than one written two centuries later by Count Nikolaus Ludwig von Zinzendorf. Here we may enter into the very heart of Luther's Reformation, one fervently joined by Calvin and those Reformed Christians who bear his name today:

> *Jesus, thy blood and righteousness*
> *My beauty are, my glorious dress*
> *'midst flaming worlds, in these arrayed*
> *with joy shall I lift up my head.*
>
> *Bold shall I stand in thy great day*
> *for who aught to my charge shall lay?*
> *Fully absolved through these I am*
> *from sin and fear, from guilt and shame.*[5]

Heads lifted up with joy, looking to the cross, and hearts lifted up with a hope of glory in the grace of Christ. This is the gospel recovered by Luther, the gospel spread throughout the world by the Reformation and its children. It is the only gospel that will give hope to our world, as we look away from ourselves and to the cross, where the Son of God died so that sinners may be saved.

THE BLOOD OF CHRIST
IN PURITAN PIETY

Joel R. Beeke

Let us look upon a crucified Christ, the remedy of all our miseries. His cross hath procured a crown, his passion hath expiated our transgression. His death hath disarmed the law, his blood hath washed a believer's soul. This death is the destruction of our enemies, the spring of our happiness, and the eternal testimony of divine love.[1]

—Stephen Charnock

Although the Puritans did not write prolifically on the doctrine of Christ's atonement as it relates to his imputed righteousness and the way that that righteousness is received by sinners through Spirit-worked faith to their justification, they took a staunchly Reformed position on this foundational issue. The reason that they were not more prolific is not hard to find: Reformers had already covered the subject thoroughly. By and large, the Puritans focused more on sanctification, that is, on living as Christians on the basis of the shed blood of Christ in every sphere of life to the glory of God. For the Puritans, this was experiential piety at its best.

In this chapter, we will examine Puritan piety in relation to the blood of Christ, specifically in Stephen Charnock's "The Cleansing

Virtue of Christ's Blood" and "The Knowledge of Christ Crucified"; Thomas Goodwin's "Reconciliation by the Blood of Christ";
and Isaac Ambrose's *Looking Unto Jesus*.[2] These writings reveal the
Puritan conviction that Christ's work outside of us (an objective,
justifying salvation) finds its counterpart within us (a subjective,
sanctifying salvation), thereby promoting an experiential piety that
lives under the shadow of the cross.

Definitions and Context

First, we should define our terms within the historical and theological
context of Puritanism. Let us look at the three terms in our title: *the
blood of Christ, Puritan*, and *piety*. For the Puritans, *the blood of
Christ* could depict (1) all the atoning sufferings of Christ endured
for sinners; (2) all his literal blood shedding, from circumcision to
death; (3) his vicarious blood shedding and intense sufferings in
Gethsemane, Gabbatha, and Golgotha; (4) his atoning crucifixion,
i.e., his blood shedding, particularly in his death; and (5) a combination of the above, with an emphasis on the substitutionary nature
of his sufferings and death. Here, we will use the fifth definition: a
combination of the other four definitions, with an emphasis on the
substitutionary nature of Christ's sufferings and death.[3]

By *Puritan*, we mean those English Christians who were dissat-
isfied with the worship and government of the Church of England
because it deviated from the pattern found in Scripture. The Puritan
movement, which lasted from the 1560s to about the 1710s, called
for the pure preaching of God's Word, for purity of worship as commanded in Scripture, for purity of church government by the replacement of the rule of bishops with Presbyterian government, and for
purity of life in Christians by obedience to God's Word.

The Puritans led people to biblical, godly living that was consistent with the Reformed doctrines of grace. Doctrinally, Puritanism
upheld a broad and vigorous Calvinism; experientially, it was a warm
and contagious Christianity; evangelistically, it was tender as well as

aggressive. Though despised and often persecuted, the Puritans had a great impact on Britain, the Netherlands, America, and other parts of the world. Many of their books are still read and treasured today because of their depth of knowledge and spiritual power.

By *piety*, we mean a childlike fear of God that combines living to the glory of God in every sphere of life with a reverential awe and zealous love for God in all his attributes. The truly pious are sensitive to God and his graciousness. They are like Moses at the burning bush in Exodus 3 and Isaiah in his vision of God in the temple in Isaiah 6. They know by experience that Jesus' atoning death, resurrection, and heavenly intercession liberate us from the slavish fear of God and promote our filial fear. They have experienced great awe, heartfelt worship, childlike confidence, prayerful submission, and profound joy in Christ. This fear is what Calvin called *pietas* (piety), and he declared it to be the heart of all true religion and the sole purpose for which he wrote his classic *Institutes*.[4]

Within their historical and theological context, the Puritans were keen to demolish the errors of the semi-Pelagian Roman Catholics, anti-Trinitarian Socinians, and free-will Arminians. They opposed Roman Catholics, such as the Jesuit preacher and professor Cardinal Robert Bellarmine (1542–1621). They rejected Socinianism, particularly the views of Laelius (1525–1562) and Faustus (1539–1604) and the Polish Racovian Catechism (1605), which expressed Socinian theology. Socinians denied Christ's deity and his death as a punishment for sin, thus opposing the foundational Reformation doctrine of justification by Christ's imputed righteousness. Some Arminians rejected the penal substitutionary view of the atonement; this rejection was developed by Hugo Grotius (1583–1645), who viewed the death of Christ as only illustrative of the punishment that rebellion against God may attract and therefore as only a deterrent in the interests of good government. Puritans also opposed the views of the Amyraldians and their hypothetical universalism, and some wrote against the neonomian views of Richard Baxter, who was a Puritan but was unsound on justification.

We will now summarize various aspects of the blood of Christ in Puritan piety and then conclude with some practical lessons that promote such piety.

Redemptive Cleansing in Christ's Incarnation and Death

For the Puritans, the truth that God found a remedy for man's sin through the incarnation and death of his Son from eternity past (before man even sinned) was astonishing cause for humility, joy, and worship. As Thomas Goodwin writes, "Before the wound [of sin] was given, [God] provided a plaster and sufficient remedy to salve all again, which otherwise had been past finding out. For we, who could never have found out a remedy for a cut finger (had not God prescribed and appointed one), could much less for this life."[5]

Christ's blood is sufficient to save the greatest of sinners from his sins. Christ's blood, Charnock writes,

> cleanseth from all sin universally. For since it was the blood of so great a person as the Son of God, it is as powerful to cleanse us from the greatest as the least. Had it been the blood of a sinful creature, it had been so far from expiation, that it would rather have been for pollution. Had it been the blood of an angel, though holy (supposing they had any to shed), yet it had been the blood of a creature, and therefore incapable of mounting to an infinite value; but since it is the blood of the Son of God, it is both the blood of a holy and of an uncreated and infinite person. Is it not therefore able to exceed all the bulk of finite sins, and to equal in dignity the infiniteness of the injury in every transgressor?[6]

The Puritans taught a threefold cleansing through the blood of Christ. First, there was an objective cleansing of believers in Christ's death and resurrection. Then they argued for a subjective cleansing the moment when the soul passes from death to life by embracing Christ's merits in faith. Finally, they asserted that there was a sensible cleansing when the Holy Spirit sprinkles Christ's blood on the soul to make the soul conscious that it is washed clean, is forgiven of all its trespasses, and has a right to eternal life. This sensible cleansing was sometimes referred to as justification in the court of conscience. In the words of Stephen Charnock:

> This cleansing from guilt may be considered as meritorious or applicative. As the blood of Christ was offered to God, this purification was meritoriously wrought; as particularly pleaded for a person, it is actually wrought; as sprinkled upon the conscience, it is sensibly wrought. The first merits the removal of guilt, the second solicits it, the third ensures it; the one was wrought upon the cross, the other is acted upon his throne, and the third pronounced in the conscience.[7]

Blood Cleansing: Three Aspects

The Puritans said that three things are involved in Christ's blood-cleansing of sin. First, there is *substitution*. In salvation, Jesus Christ takes our place, assuming our demerits and giving us all his merits. Again Charnock notes:

> He received our evils to bestow his good, and submitted to our curse to impart to us his blessings; sustained the extremity of that wrath we had deserved, to confer upon us the grace he had purchased. The sin in us, which he was free from, was by divine estimation transferred upon him, as if he were guilty, that the righteousness he has, which we were destitute of, might be transferred upon us, as if we were innocent. He was made sin, as if he had sinned all the sins of men, and we are made righteousness, as if we had not sinned at all.[8]

Second, there is *imputation*, which is closely related to substitution, though it looks at substitution in a more forensic or judicial way. Imputation is the belief that God reckons the unrighteousness of the ungodly to Christ's account and the righteousness of Christ to the ungodly sinner's account. As Charnock writes:

We are not righteous before God by an inherent, but by an imputed
righteousness, nor was Christ made sin by inherent, but imputed,
guilt. The same way that his righteousness is communicated to us,
our sin was communicated to him. Righteousness was inherent
in him, but imputed to us; sin was inherent in us, but imputed to
him.[9]

Imputation is possible through our legal and covenantal union
with Christ, much as the imputation of Adam's sin is grounded in
our seminal and covenantal union with him. Charnock explains:

If we had not had a union with Adam in nature, and been seminally in him, his sin could no more have been imputed to us
than the sin of the fallen angels could be counted ours; so if we
have not a union with Christ, his righteousness can no more
be reckoned to us than the righteousness of the standing angels
can be imputed to us. We must therefore be in Christ as really
as we were in Adam, though not in the same manner of reality.
We were in Adam seminally, we are in Christ legally; yet so that
it is counted in the judgment of God as much as if there were a
seminal union. Believers are therefore called the seed of Christ,
Isa. liii.10, Ps. xxii.30.[10]

Third, there is *justification*, which consists of the forgiveness of
sins and a right to eternal life. Christ's complete blood atonement
(his passive obedience) and perfect law-obedience (his active obedience) fully satisfy God's offended justice. This twofold obedience
provides full justification, which the sinner receives by faith. Christ's
blood atonement is the ground of the sinner's forgiveness of sins,
"yet actual pardon is not bestowed without believing."[11] Charnock
comments on this:

A *not guilty* is entered into the court of God when this blood is
pleaded, and a *not guilty* upon the roll of conscience when this
blood is sprinkled. It appeaseth God's justice and quencheth wrath.
As it is pleaded before his tribunal, it silenceth the accusations of

sin; and quells tumults in a wrangling conscience, as it is sprinkled upon the soul.[12]

Christ's obedience to the law is the ground of the sinner's right to eternal life. Charnock says: "Since the law is not abrogated [by the fall of man], it must be exactly obeyed, the honour of it must be preserved; it cannot be observed by us, it was Christ only who kept it, and never broke it, and endured the penalty of it for us, not for himself." The virtue of Christ's perfect obedience "must be transferred to us, which cannot be any other way than by imputation, or reckoning it ours, as we are one body with him."[13]

As Thomas Goodwin concludes: "By this his both active and passive obedience, through the acceptation of his person, who performed it, he [Jesus] hath completed the work of reconciliation with his Father."[14]

Not everyone agreed with this view, especially not the Socinians. Isaac Ambrose notes of their opposition:

A great controversy is of late risen up, "Whether Christ's death be a satisfaction to divine justice?" But the very words "redeeming and buying," do plainly demonstrate, that a satisfaction was given to God by the death of Jesus, "He gave himself for us that he might redeem us," Tit. 2:14. Ye are bought with a price, 1 Cor. 6:20. And what price was that? Why, his own blood. "Thou wast slain, and hast redeemed us to God by thy blood," Rev. 5:9, (i.e.) by thy death and passion. This was the (*lutron*), that ransom which Christ gave for his elect. "The Son of man came to give himself a ransom for many," Matt. 20:28, or as the apostle, "He gave himself a ransom for all," 1 Tim. 2:6, the word is here (*antilutron*), which signifies an adequate price, or a counter-price; as when one doeth or undergoeth something in the room of another; as when one yields himself a captive for the redeeming of another out of captivity, or gives up his own life for the saving of another man's life; so Christ gave himself (*antilutron*) a ransom, or counter-price, submitting himself to the like punishment that his redeemed ones should have undergone.[15]

Ambrose thus warns about the danger of separating Christ's active and passive obedience:

> If Christ's death be mine, then is Christ's life mine. Christ's active and passive obedience cannot be severed; Christ is not divided: we must not seek one part of our righteousness in his birth, another in his habitual holiness, another in the integrity of his life, another in his obedience unto death. They that endeavor to separate Christ's active and passive obedience, they do exceedingly derogate from Christ, and make him but half a Saviour: was not Christ our surety? Heb. 7:22, and thereupon was he not bound to fulfil all righteousness for us? (*i.e.*) As to suffer in our stead, so to obey in our stead. Oh! take heed of opposing or separating Christ's death and Christ's life; either we have all Christ, or we have no part in Christ.[16]

Faith in the Blood

By faith, Christ's blood is received and sprinkled on the believer's conscience by the Spirit of Christ. In this act of faith, the sinner is made willing, says Charnock,

> to receive Christ upon the terms he is offered. Since a mediator is not a mediator of one, but supposeth in the notion of it two parties, there must be a consent on both sides. God's consent is manifested by giving, our consent is by receiving, which is a title given to faith, John 1:12; God's consent in appointing and accepting the atonement, and ours in receiving the atonement, which is all one with "receiving forgiveness of sin," Rom. 5:11.[17]

Given the infinite value of Christ's atoning blood, no sin should stand in the way of the sinner's reception of mercy by faith. Charnock puts this quaintly: "The nature of the sins, and the blackness of them, is not regarded, when this blood is set in opposition to them. God only looks at what the sinners are, whether they repent and believe." He goes on to say that justification by faith through Christ's blood is sufficient for all sin, "the sins of all believing persons in all parts, in all ages of the world, from the first moment of man's sinning, to the last sin committed on the earth."[18]

Charnock more precisely explains the role of faith in justification:

> This faith is not our righteousness, nor is it ever called so, but we have a righteousness by the means of faith. *By* faith, or *through* faith, is the language of the apostle: Romans 3:22, 25, "Faith in his blood," faith reaching out to his blood, embracing his blood, sucking up his propitiating blood and pleading it. Though faith is the eye and hand of the soul, looking up and reaching out to [the] whole Christ as offered in the promise, yet in this act of it to be freed from the guilt of sin, it grasps Christ as a sacrifice, it hangs upon him as paying a price, and takes this blood as a blood shed for the soul, and insists upon the sufficient value of it with God. . . . [So] we are *justified by faith,* not that *faith justifies us.* The efficacy is in Christ's blood, the reception of it in our faith (Rom. 5:1).[19]

Charnock stresses the sufficiency of Christ's blood received by faith by pointing out:

> The first sin we read of cleansed by this blood, after it was shed, was the most prodigious wickedness that ever was committed in the face of the sun, even the murder of the Son of God, Acts 2:36, 38. So that, suppose a man were able to pull heaven and earth to pieces, murder all the rest of mankind, destroy the angels, those superlative arts of the creation, he would not contract so monstrous a guilt as those did in the crucifying the Son of God, whose person was infinitely superior to the whole creation. God then hereby gave an experiment of the inestimable value of Christ's blood, and the inexhaustible virtue of it. Well might the apostle say, "The blood of Christ cleanseth us from all sin."[20]

Sanctification through the Blood

Christ's blood was shed not only for justification but also for sanctification. As Charnock points out:

There is a cleansing from *guilt*, and a cleansing from *filth*; both are the fruits of this blood: the guilt is removed by remission, the filth by purification. Christ doth both: he cleanseth us from our guilt as he is our righteousness, from our spot as he is our sanctification; for he is both to us, 1 Cor. 1:30, the one upon the account of his merit, the other by his efficacy, which he exerts by his Spirit.[21]

The knowledge of Christ crucified sanctifies us in several ways. Charnock mentions five.

First, the knowledge of Christ crucified sanctifies us by enlivening our *repentance*. We cannot look on the blood of Christ without grieving that our sins nailed him to the cross and brought on his bloodshed. "Should we not bleed as often as we seriously thought of Christ's bleeding for us?" asks Charnock. This grief, in turn, makes us detest our sin. "It is a 'look upon Christ pierced' that pierceth the soul, Zech. 12:10. Would not this blood acquaint us that the malignity of sin was so great, that it could not be blotted out by the blood of the whole creation! Would it not astonish us that none had strength enough to match it, but one equal with God! Would not such an astonishment break out into penitent reflections!"[22]

Second, the knowledge of Christ crucified sanctifies us by enlivening our *faith*. "When we behold a Christ crucified, how can we distrust God, that hath in that, as a plain tablet write this language, that he will spare nothing for us, since he hath not spared the best he had. What greater assurance can he give? Where is there anything in heaven or earth that can be a greater pledge of his affection?"[23]

Third, the knowledge of Christ crucified sanctifies us by enlivening our *prayer*. "We should think of it every time we go to God in prayer [that] it was by this death the throne of God was opened. This will chase away that fear that disarms us of our vigour [in prayer]. It will compose our souls to offer up delightful petitions."[24]

Fourth, the knowledge of Christ crucified sanctifies us by enlivening our *holiness*. "We should see no charms in sin that may not be overcome by that ravishing love which bubbles up in every drop of the Redeemer's blood. Can we, with lively thoughts of this, sin against so much tenderness, compassion, grace, and the other perfections of God, which sound so loudly in our ears from the cross of Jesus? Shall we consider him hanging there to deliver us from hell, and yet retain any spirit to walk in the way which leads thereto?"

Charnock then becomes even more direct: "Shall we see him groaning in our place and stead, and dare to tell him by our unworthy carriage that we regard him not, and that he might have spared his pains? . . . Can we take any pleasure in that which procured so much pain to our best friend?" Charnock concludes that when we do not meditate on Christ's substitutionary blood, we are prone to continue in sin, as if Christ died to give us a license to sin rather than to destroy sin. On the other hand, daily regarding his blood will stifle the worldliness and ungodliness that harasses our souls.[25]

Finally, the knowledge of Christ crucified sanctifies us by enlivening our *comfort*. "What comfort can be wanting when we look upon Christ crucified as our surety, and look upon ourselves as crucified in him; when we consider our sins as punished in him, and ourselves accepted by virtue of his cross." Charnock then summarizes these comforts:

> Let us look upon a crucified Christ, the remedy of all our miseries. His cross hath procured a crown, his passion hath expiated our transgression. His death hath disarmed the law, his blood hath washed a believer's soul. This death is the destruction of our enemies, the spring of our happiness, and the eternal testimony of divine love.[26]

Victory through the Blood

The believer may know victory through Christ's blood already in this life in terms of sin's "condemnation and punishment." His sin is blotted out of "the book of God's justice; it is no more to be remembered in a way of legal and judicial sentence against the sinner. Though the nature of sin doth not cease to be sinful, yet the power of sin ceaseth to be condemning. The sentence of the law is revoked, the right to condemn is removed, and sin is not imputed to them, 1 Corinthians 5:19."[27]

But that does not mean that the blood of Christ cleanses us perfectly in the here and now from all consciousness of sin and the stirrings of sin. Believers "need a daily pardon upon daily sin." Yet the believer is on his way to victory in his ongoing battles with sin. Charnock describes this graphically:

> Some sparks of the fiery law will sometimes flash in our consciences, and the peace of the gospel be put under a veil. The smiles of God's countenance seem to be changed into frowns, and the blood of Christ appears as if it ran low. Evidences may be blurred and guilt revived. Satan may accuse, and conscience knows not how to answer him. The sore may run fresh in the night, and the soul have not only comfort hid from it, but refuse comfort when it stands at the door. There will be startlings of unbelief, distrusts of God, and misty steams from the miry lake of nature.

He goes on to say:

> But it hath laid a perfect foundation, and the top stone of a full sense and comfort will be laid at last. Peace shall be as an illustrious sunshine without a cloud, a triumphant breaking out of love, without any arrows of wrath sticking fast in the conscience; a sweet calm, without any whisper of a blustering tempest; the guilt of sin shall be for ever wiped out of the conscience, as well as blotted out of God's book. The accuser shall no more accuse us, either to God or ourselves; no new indictment shall be formed by him at the bar of conscience; nay, conscience itself shall be for ever purged, and sing an uninterrupted *requiem*, and hymn of peace, shall not hiss the least accusation of a crime. As God's justice shall read nothing for condemnation, so conscience shall read nothing for accusation. The blood of Christ will be perfect in the effects of it. As it rent the veil between God and us, it will rend the veil between conscience and us; no more frowns from the one, nor any more janglings in the other.[28]

Charnock then concludes: "The blood of Christ shall still the waves, and expel the filth, and crown the soul with an everlasting victory. 'The spirits of just men' are then 'made perfect,' Hebrews 12:23."[29]

Heavenly Joy through the Blood

The Puritans loved meditating on heaven; no subject is mentioned more frequently in all their tomes. Heaven, says Charnock, is

> cemented and prepared by the blood of Christ. By the law against sin we were to have our bodies reduced to dust, and our souls lie under the sentence of the wrath of God. But our crucified Saviour hath purchased the redemption of our body, to be evidenced by a resurrection, Romans 8:23, and a standing security of our souls in a place of bliss, to which believer shall have a real ascent, and in which they shall have a local residence, which is called the purchased possession. . . . We lost a paradise by sin, and have gained a heaven by the cross.[30]

Ambrose puts it this way:

> It is the blood of Christ that rends the veil, and makes a way into the holy of holies, that is, into the kingdom of heaven; without this blood there is no access to God; it is only by the blood of Christ that heaven is open to our prayers, and that heaven is open to our persons. This blood is the key that unlocks heaven, and lets in the souls of his redeemed ones.[31]

Practical Lessons That Promote Piety

The Puritans offer the following practical lessons learned from the atoning blood of Christ to promote piety.

1) If we are not saved personally by Christ's blood, we are on our way to condemnation. No one who lacks a saving interest in the cleansing blood for his own soul will ever be delivered from his guilt. He will remain unconverted as long as he remains in this condition.

Charnock writes, "The blood of Christ is so far from cleansing an unbeliever from all sin, that it rather binds his sins the faster on him. Unbelief locks the sins on more strongly, so that the violations of the law stick closer to him, and the wrath of God hangs over him."[32]

2) God's mercy is administered only on the basis of Christ's blood. "No freedom from the guilt of sin is to be expected from mere mercy," says Charnock. He further emphasizes that the high priest could not approach the mercy seat in the Old Testament era without blood (Deut. 9:7), and "Christ himself, typified by the high priest, expects no mercy for any of his followers, but by the merit of his blood."[33] God's mercy is just mercy.

Christ's blood is the only way of justification and salvation. Because all that we think, say, and do by nature is tainted with sin, everything we do adds to our condemnation. Since none of our works is perfect, none is justifying. All that we do comes short of the glory of God (Rom. 3:23). God's way of justifying sinners strips us of all glory in ourselves or our own righteousness.

3) Our hope for salvation rests in Christ's righteousness being imputed to us. How comforting it is to know and experience that the blood of Jesus Christ cleanses—makes absolutely pure—from all—yes, *all*—sin. No sinner can ever say that Christ's satisfaction is not sufficient to annul his sin. Isaac Ambrose asserts that Christ's satisfaction is not only "copious and full," but that his "death and blood is superabundant to our sins: 'The grace of our Lord was exceeding abundant [*hyperepleonasen*],' 1 Tim. 1:14, it was over full, redundant, more than enough." He goes on to say:

> Many an humble soul is apt enough to complain, "Oh! if I had not been so great a sinner, if I had not committed such and such transgressions there might have been hope." This is to undervalue Christ's redemption; this is to think there is more in sin to damn, than in Christ's sufferings to save, whereas all thy sins to Christ are but as a little cloud to the glorious sun, yea, all the sins of all the men in the world, are but to Christ's merits as a drop to the ocean.

I speak this not to encourage the presumptuous sinner, for alas, he hath no part in this satisfaction, but to comfort the humbled sinner, who is loadened with a sense of his sins; what though they were a burden greater than he can bear, yet they are not a burden greater than Christ can bear. There is in Christ's blood an infinite treasure, able to sanctify thee and all the world; there is in Christ's death a ransom, a counter-price sufficient to redeem all the sinners that ever were or ever shall be.[34]

4) Christ's bloody satisfaction should make us deeply mourn over our sin that nailed him to the cross. Isaac Ambrose is typical of the Puritans on this subject:

O the curse and bitterness that our sins have brought on Jesus Christ! When I but think of these bleeding veins, bruised shoulders, scourged sides, furrowed back, harrowed temples, digged hands and feet, and then consider that my sins were the cause of all; methinks I should need no more arguments for self-abhorring! Christians, would not your hearts rise against him that should kill your father, mother, brother, wife, husband; dearest relations in all the world! O then, how should your hearts and souls rise against sin? Surely your sin it was, that murdered Christ, that killed him, who is instead of all relations, who is a thousand, thousand times dearer to you, than father, mother, husband, child, or whomsoever; one thought of this should, methinks, be enough to make you say, as Job did, "I abhor myself, and repent in dust and ashes," Job 42:9. Oh! what is that cross on the back of Christ? My sins; oh! what is that crown on the head of Christ? My sins; oh! what is the nail in the right-hand, and that other in the left-hand of Christ? My sins; oh! what is that spear in the side of Christ? My sins; what are those nails and wounds in the feet of Christ? My sins . . . oh my sins, my sins, my sins![35]

5) No one who comes to Christ by faith and repentance shall be turned away. To those who fear that Christ will not accept them because they are full of sin and have flagrantly sinned against him for so many decades, Thomas Goodwin says: "The text [Colossians

1:20] tells us, that 'Christ hath all fullness in him to reconcile'; and till thou canst be fuller of sin than he of righteousness, there is enough to pardon thee: 'He is able to save to the utmost,' be the case never so bad, the matter never so foul. . . . Consider that this fullness . . . hath resided longer in Christ . . . than sin hath done in thee; yea, it will dwell in him for ever, it is an everlasting righteousness." No matter how bad your heart and your record are, says Goodwin, "thou art the welcomer if thou wilt but come to him," for he delights to save the chiefest of sinners.[36]

6) Let us aspire after the blood of Christ more fervently and consistently. Pray for this inclination daily, says Ambrose; he then adds: "Oh, my Jesus! that thou wouldst breed in me ardent desires, vehement longings; unutterable groans, mighty gaspings: O that I were like the dry and thirsty ground that gapes and cleaves, and opens for drops of rain! When my spirit is in right frame, I feel some desires after Christ's blood, but how short are these desires? How unworthy of the things desired? Come, Lord, kindle in me hot, burning desires, and then give me the desirable object."

Are you washed in Christ's blood? If not, ask God to show you your malady and fly to Christ's blood today for your only remedy. And, dear believers, "since we contract guilt every day, let us daily apply the medicine." Let none of us rest without experiencing every day that "the blood of Jesus Christ cleanseth us from all sin."[37] Such experience, after all, is the goal of Puritan piety—living every day in the shadow of the cross.

POST-REFORMATION DEVELOPMENTS IN THE DOCTRINE OF THE ATONEMENT

Carl R. Trueman

An important thing to understand about Protestantism is that the Reformation was a pastoral revolution. As we focus on the atonement, we are considering what one might call an objective, doctrinal concept. But we must never lose sight of the fact that the Reformation was a movement, or a series of movements, borne out of pastoral concerns.

Supremely, of course, we see this in the life of Martin Luther. Prior to 1517, the year traditionally seen as marking the beginning of the Reformation in Wittenberg, the burning question for Luther was, "How can I find a gracious God?" It was as he made the breakthrough to understand that God reveals himself as gracious only in and through his incarnation, and specifically as he dies incarnate upon the cross, that Luther was able to answer this question and resolve this most pressing pastoral concern. Thus, in Luther's thought there is an intimate, unbreakable connection between Christ's objective atonement and the believer's subjective assurance.

The Three Forms of Unity

The connection between Christ's objective atonement and the believer's subjective assurance is maintained in the basic confessional documents that flow from the Reformation. Consider the Heidelberg Catechism, Question 1. The Heidelberg Catechism is, along with the Belgic Confession and the Canons of Dordt, one of the so-called Three Forms of Unity that the continental Reformed churches, and those American churches who look to mainland Europe for their origins, use as their confessional basis. In America, this would include the Christian Reformed Church, the United Reformed Church, the Reformed Church of America, and the Reformed Church in the United States.

The Heidelberg Catechism

The Heidelberg Catechism was a Reformed catechism put together during the 1560s in the German city of that name, and it is well known for its pastoral tone and approach. Here is how that catechism begins in "Lord's Day, Question 1":

> Question: What is your only comfort in life and death? Answer: That I with body and soul both in life and death am not my own but belong unto my faithful Savior, Jesus Christ, who with His precious blood has fully satisfied all my sins and delivered me from all the power of the devil, and so preserves me, that without the will of my Heavenly Father, not a hair can fall from my head. Yea, but all things must be subservient to my salvation. Wherefore, by His Holy Spirit, He also assures me of eternal life and makes me heartily willing and ready henceforth to live with Him.

We see in the first part of that answer, "That I with body and soul both in life and death am not my own but belong onto my faithful Savior, Jesus Christ, who with His precious blood has fully satisfied all my sins and delivered me from all the power of the devil," a definite connection between the atonement of the Lord Jesus Christ and Christian experience. This central Protestant doctrine, that the individual believer can be assured that God is gracious toward him, is deeply rooted in the teaching of Christ's atonement on the cross of Calvary.

The Belgic Confession

If we turn to another of the three forms of unity, the Belgic Confession, we will find the same connection being struck again:

> We believe that Jesus Christ is ordained with an oath to be an everlasting high priest after the order of Melchisedek, and that He has presented Himself in our behalf before the Father, to appease His wrath by His full satisfaction by offering Himself on the tree of the cross and pouring out His precious blood to purge away our sins as the prophets foretold. For it is written, He was wounded for our transgressions, He was bruised for our iniquities, the chastisement of our peace was upon Him, and with His stripes we are healed. He was led as a lamb to the slaughter and numbered with the transgressors, and condemned by Pontius Pilate as a malefactor, though he first declared Him innocent. Therefore He restored that which He took not away, and suffered the righteous for the unrighteous, as well in His body as in His soul, feeling the terrible punishment which our sins had merited. . . . Wherefore we justly say with the Apostle Paul that we know nothing save Jesus Christ and Him crucified. We count all things but loss and refuse for the excellency of the knowledge of Christ Jesus our Lord in whose wounds we find all manner of consolation. Neither is it necessary to seek or invent any other means of being reconciled to God than this only sacrifice, once suffered but which He had perfected forever for them that are sanctified. This also is the reason why He was called by the angel of God Jesus, that is to say Savior, because He would save His people from their sins. (chap. 21)

What we see in the Belgic Confession, as in the Heidelberg Catechism, is the crucial importance of the finality of Christ's sacrifice on Calvary as undergirding and supporting the central Protestant doctrine that the individual believer can be assured that God is gracious to him. This is why, during the Reformation and in the years after the

Reformation, debates over the doctrine of atonement were not simply ivory-tower discussions among hair-splitting theologians. Rather, their discussion was deeply grounded in the pastoral life of the church. The Reformers understood that if you tinker with the atonement, if you change your understanding of Christ's sacrifice, then you must of necessity change your understanding of Christian assurance.

This, of course, connects to one of the other great Protestant doctrines, justification by grace through faith. The whole point of the Protestant understanding of faith was that faith is not a work. Faith does not make up for something lacking in the sacrifice of Christ. In no way does our assurance depend ultimately upon our subjective faith. Faith is merely the passive instrument whereby the joy, the good news, and the objective benefit of Christ's sacrifice can be appropriated by the individual.

This connection between the cross and Christian experience is why issues relating to Christ's precious blood, to Christ's atonement, were a high priority in the minds of the Reformers and of Protestants who look to the Reformation for their inspiration. The reason for this priority is the important connection between the doctrine of the atonement and the pastoral needs faced in the local church. In the Reformation Protestant mind-set, the connection between atonement and Christian experience is unbreakable and absolutely central.

Post-Reformation Challenges to the Atonement

Understanding the pastoral importance of the atonement provides a context for us to consider a number of challenges that the Protestant doctrine faced in the years after the Reformation. Protestantism did not just appear out of nowhere in 1517 and reach some kind of final codification in the 1560s with the production of the Belgic Confession and the Heidelberg Catechism. Protestantism continued to develop because there continued to be, throughout the sixteenth and seventeenth centuries, significant external and internal challenges to many of its positions.

For example, the whole matter of assurance became highly contested, and this was, as one might expect, a uniquely Protestant problem. (One can only start having a problem with Christian assurance when first asking questions about Christian assurance. If you start asking questions about Christian assurance only at the Reformation, you are going to find answers being given to the problems surrounding that question only in the years subsequent to it.) It is much the same with the atonement. As challenges were launched against its various positions from both within and without Protestantism, Protestants themselves began to refine and reflect on the nature of the atonement and its connection to Christian experience in more detail than we find in the Heidelberg Catechism and the Belgic Confession in the 1560s.

There were four main challenges in the late sixteenth and the seventeenth centuries to the confessional or classic Protestant position set down in the Heidelberg Catechism and the Belgic Confession.

The Roman Challenge

The first challenge came from the Roman Catholic Church. The primary problem that Reformation Protestants would have with Catholicism on the issue of atonement was the mass. If the mass is, in some sense, a repetition of the sacrifice of Christ every Sunday, then how can one have assurance? How can one be confident that the sacrifice has been applied appropriately and definitively to oneself, if it must always be repeated? Moreover, why can't there be a single mass of infinite value on one Sunday at some point in time that deals with all the sins of the world?

From a Protestant perspective, the very repetition of the mass as an ongoing sacrifice seems to strike at the all-sufficient nature of the once-for-all death of the Lord Jesus Christ. The Roman Catholic challenge, of course, was there right from the beginning. Luther's theology was in large part a rebellion against the sacramental system of the medieval church.

The Arminian Challenge

More dangerous from a Protestant perspective was the Arminian challenge. Arminians today are those nice Christian people who think, among other things, that the doctrine of predestination is unfair. They have a gut reaction against Reformed theology and, therefore, develop a fairly simple and straightforward theology that simply rejects predestination.

But Arminianism in the sixteenth and seventeenth centuries was a much more sophisticated and complicated phenomenon. It took its cue from the Dutchman, Jacob Arminius (1559–1609). He had been a pupil of Theodore Beza, Calvin's successor in Geneva, but had increasingly come to reject his teacher's predestinarian views. However, as an astute and very thoughtful theologian, Arminius knew that one could not make a modification in one point of the Reformed system without having correlative changes elsewhere.

When it came to the death of Christ, Arminius detached Christ's death from the decree of election. He did not, as popularly thought, reject the decree of election, but he understood it in a particularly clever and subtle way. What he did was to reconstruct it on what theologians would call a semi-Pelagian basis.

But the real significance of his work, for this discussion, is the fact that he effectively detached the atonement from the decree. In other words, whereas the Heidelberg Catechism and the Belgic Confession talk about the finality of Christ's death on the cross at Calvary as actually accomplishing salvation for particular, individual believers—that is, for the elect—Arminius and his followers turned the cross from the achievement of salvation into something that provided merely the objective basis for forgiveness. In other words, because Christ had died, it merely became possible for God to forgive anyone their sin. Christ's death in itself had an infinite value, and it was up to God to set conditions after the death of Christ, logically speaking, as to how the benefits of Christ's death would be applied to individuals.

In addition to this, Arminius increasingly focused Christ's work as mediator on his *suffering* from Gethsemane onwards rather than on his positive *obedience* to God's law. The Reformed traditionally saw—and see—Christ's work of mediation as involving the whole of his life. There was a positive fulfillment of the law up until the point where Christ was handed over in the garden to the Roman and Jewish authorities. Then there is a kind of passive suffering that Christ undergoes on behalf of his people.

Theologians typically use a rather unfortunate set of terms for this distinction: active righteousness or active obedience, meaning Christ's active obedience of the law, and passive righteousness or passive obedience, meaning Christ's submission to suffering at the hands of the authorities. The word *passive* is unfortunate because it implies that Christ was not active in his forbearance and his suffering on the cross, which he obviously was. But the distinction is now deeply embedded in Reformed theology and to an extent it is a very useful one.

Arminius, however, wanted to argue that Christ's mediation, his work as mediator, was focused exclusively upon his suffering, that is, upon his passive obedience and righteousness. As a correlative issue, Arminius wanted to turn justification from being the imputation of Christ's righteousness into merely the remission of the believer's sins, hence leaving a space open in justification for the believer to be actually righteous and to "make up" what we might with some crudity describe as a shortfall in righteousness.

Arminianism rose up from within Protestantism, and for this reason it was peculiarly dangerous. It used the same basic principles as Reformed Protestants did for constructing its theology: Scripture alone as the sole cognitive foundation for theology. Thus, it differed from the threat coming from Roman Catholicism. After all, Protestants could always point the finger at Catholicism and say that the difference between the two traditions was that Protestants formulate their theology on the basis of Scripture alone, while Catholics have this extra-Scriptural tradition that they believe is decisive in the formulation of doctrine. But Arminians could affirm sola scriptura, making their challenge significantly more difficult to deflect.

The Amyraldian Challenge

The third challenge was another that arose from within Protestantism. This was the Amyraldian challenge. Amyraldianism takes its name from Moses Amyraut (1596–1664), a French theologian who taught at the School of Saumur in France. He was a Protestant and a very clever and astute theologian.

Reformed scholastics in the seventeenth century always considered Amyraldianism to be qualitatively different from Arminianism. In the late 1960s, a scholar named Brian Armstrong authored a work titled *Calvinism and the Amyraut Heresy*. It is the only book of which I am aware where this historical error is made in the very title. Amyraldianism was not generally regarded by the Reformed Orthodox in the seventeenth century as a heresy; it was regarded as an error, and the difference is crucial. Arminianism was regarded as a heresy. Certain aspects of Roman Catholicism were regarded as heresy by the Reformed.

The Reformed did not regard the particular view of atonement that the Amyraldians held as completely vitiating their theology. Often seventeenth-century Reformed Orthodox figures, such as John Owen or Frances Turretin, would be very critical of Amyraut and his followers, but they would always treat them as Christian brothers and would often lavish praise on them at those points where they agreed. They would never use language that implied that the Amyraldians were anything other than mistaken Christian brothers. (Arminianism, Catholicism, and Socinianism, which we have next to consider, were different. The Reformed regarded them as heretical movements.)

What was Amyraldianism then? The Amyraldians argued for a different ordering of the decrees in God. Typical Reformed Orthodoxy ordered the decrees in the mind of God. It is important to remember that we are talking about a logical ordering, not a chronological one. There is no succession in God, so we are not talking about God moving through time and setting up this decree at one point in time and another decree at another point in time. This is a purely logical ordering: which decree logically presupposes which other decree in the mind of God?

A typical Orthodox Reformed ordering of the decrees such as an infralapsarian ordering would go something like this: God decrees creation; God decrees the fall; God decrees election and reprobation; God decrees that Christ will be mediator on behalf of the elect. So you have an order of creation, fall, election/reprobation, and the appointment of Christ as mediator. Then it would often be argued that because the appointment of Christ as mediator was logically subsequent to the decree of election/reprobation, Christ was therefore only appointed as mediator for those whom God had first of all (logically speaking) elected to save. This leads to what we now call the classic doctrine of limited atonement.

This doctrine has, of course, raised perennial questions, the most pressing of which is this: how can you tell a nonbeliever, "Christ died for you," when you don't know that Christ *did* die for him? If we believe the decree of election is logically prior to the decree of Christ as mediator, we can't say to a person who is not a professing Christian that Christ died for him. Thus, it would be seen by some, understandably, as having a profound impact upon how one would preach the gospel and evangelize.

R. T. Kendall

R. T. Kendall, one of the successors of Martyn Lloyd-Jones at Westminster Chapel, London, wrote a historical book on this and has since articulated the Amyraldian position in a very winsome way in a series of books on preaching and evangelism. He argues that you can only preach the gospel effectively if you reject the classic Reformed ordering of the decrees and come up with something that allows you to say to the unbeliever, "Christ died for you."

So what does Amyraldianism do with the decrees to circumvent this supposed problem? The answer is that Amyraut changed the order of the decrees. You have to remember, of course, that neither Amyraldianism nor Reformed Orthodoxy is an absolutely monolithic entity and that there is always some variety within these broad traditions. So I want to give a typical example of how an Amyraldian might construct the decrees, and I hope to do so without implying that everything which goes by the name *Amyraldian* would hold to this in every detail.

An Amyraldian might construct the decrees first with the decree of creation, followed by the decree of the fall, and then by the decree that appoints Christ as mediator. Then, on the basis of that, comes the decree of election. You see what this Amyraldian ordering does? It flips the decree of election and the decree of appointing Christ as mediator such that Christ is appointed mediator potentially for everybody, prior to any particularity in election, and it is only logically subsequent to this that mediation becomes focused or comes into relation with the decree of election.

This broader picture is often nuanced in the details. R. T. Kendall makes a distinction within the sacrifice of Christ himself, arguing that while Christ does not die for a specific group but for everyone, he intercedes at the right hand of the Father only for the elect. The advantage of this position is that it allows us to tell the unbeliever we meet on the street on Sunday when we come out of church, "Christ died for you," and be confident that we speak the truth.

This position is superficially appealing, but it brings its own particular problems. If you go to your pastor and say, "Pastor, I'm struggling with lack of assurance," your pastor can now say to you, "Well, Christ died for you." Superficially, this would seem to solve your problem. But if you know your Amyraldian theology well and are astute enough, you are going to say to your pastor, "Well, yes, I know that, but is he interceding for me?" Then your pastor faces the same problem with regard to the efficacy of Christ's work as does the one holding to limited atonement.

So one of my criticisms of R. T. Kendall is his attempt to ground evangelism and assurance in the universal objective atonement of Christ. What he actually does is simply shift the nature of the crucial questions from Calvary to the right hand of God the Father in heaven. In this way, the contrast between Reformed Orthodoxy and Amyraldianism highlights once again the connection between atonement and questions of Christian assurance.

The Socinian Challenge

The fourth challenge is, in some ways, the most dangerous, and it was the one that seventeenth-century Reformed Orthodoxy spent the most time trying to refute. This is the challenge of the Socinians. Socinianism is a movement that takes its name from the life and work of two Italians, an uncle and a nephew, Laelio and Fausto Sozzini. The Latin singular of their surname was Socinus, and from this we get the English word for the movement which they inspired, Socinianism.

Socinianism arose out of Protestantism and was, in some ways, Protestantism extended to the nth degree. Socinians took very seriously the Scripture principle, and they argued that it was not enough simply to go back and correct the creedal tradition of the church in light of Scripture. It was not enough to work with the hermeneutic of trust that was typical of the magisterial Protestants in relation to the early church creeds—the belief that, by and large, the church got most issues right over the centuries, while bringing church tradition into relation with the Scripture led to some modifications but not its wholesale overthrow.

Instead, the Socinians were much more radical. They wanted to take the church back to year zero. They wanted to get rid of the early church creeds and confessions. They wanted to go back to the beginning and build their theology from the bottom up. They wanted nothing but the Bible.

It is interesting to note that there is a strange but potent similarity between some strands of modern evangelicalism and this attitude of the Socinians. Some evangelicals seem to want to reject all tradition and just sit and read their Bible. One might facetiously comment that, of course, unless they are reading it in the Hebrew and Greek, they are still connected to some tradition of Bible translation. Still, those individuals who just want to build their theology on the Bible, however orthodox in their intentions, are methodologically like the Socinians. The Socinians just had their Bible and just built their theology from the Bible.

The Socinians combined this biblicism with a very literal hermeneutic. It is often said that Socinianism represents a rationalist movement within Christianity, but it certainly did not start that way. It started as a biblical literalist *anti-metaphysical* movement, committed to purging theology of Greek philosophical language along with anything other than a literal reading of Scripture. This leads to some bizarre ideas.

To show you how non-rationalist it is, consider this example: if, like the Socinians, you reject the deity of Christ, you solve certain difficult passages in Scripture, such as those passages where Christ does not seem to know things that perhaps you think he should know if he is God. Why, after all, does Jesus not know everything, if he is divine? Those passages can give you some pause for thought, but if you do not think he is God, there is no problem.

Yet the solving of problems in one area is more than balanced by the creation of problems elsewhere. If, like the Socinians, you reject the essential deity of Christ, other passages become a problem to you. For example, in some passages Christ seems to know things that, humanly speaking, he could not possibly know. Some of the Socinians solved that problem by saying that Christ was virtually "beamed up" to heaven and supplied with this missing information during a face-to-face encounter with God before being beamed back down.

Now, whatever else that is, it is not a rationalist argument or a solution to the problem and thus should qualify any description of Socinianism, at least in its earliest phase, as a rationalist movement. Thus, Socinianism is best described not so much as rationalist as anti-metaphysical and literalist in a way that led it to reconstruct the doctrine of God in a Unitarian fashion, supported by its repudiation of Greek metaphysical vocabulary and of the early church creeds.

The Socinian Reconstruction

The most significant theological contribution of Socinianism was its reconstruction of the doctrine of God on a Unitarian basis. It is not surprising that modern Unitarianism is the intellectual descendant of Socinianism and has, historically, traced it roots to the work of the Sozzinis. A few years ago I had to get hold of a copy of the Racovian Catechism, the major Socinian Catechism of the early seventeenth century, and I was interested (though not surprised) to note that the English translation was published by, of all people, the Unitarian Society. The connections—theological and historical—are obvious.

Of course, if you reconstruct your doctrine of God as the Socinians did, you also need to reconstruct your understanding of Christ. Christ cannot be essentially God if God is one. For Socinians, Christ earns the right to be called God by living a life of perfect submission and obedience. This Christology is what theologians would call adoptionist and exemplary. Christ is *adopted* as God because of his obedience, and even then he is not God in the same sense as God the Father is God. Likewise, the saving power of Christ lies not in any objective work on our behalf, as our representative, but in his role as moral *example* of what a perfect life looks like. It lies simply in the fact that he patterns for us a life of utter, unconditional, absolute devotion to God.

Underlying Socinian reconstruction of Christology, there are
two concerns I might identify. First, there is an obvious concern for
practical morality. I often tell students that when you are dealing
with a heretical movement, the first thing to realize is that ninety-nine
out of a hundred heresies have a legitimate concern and a legitimate
question that lies behind them. The legitimate concern and question
behind the Socinian view of Christ is this: where do good works fit
into the Christian life? How does Christ connect to good works? The
answer they give is a wrong one and wholly inadequate, but their
legitimate concern was to provide a solid basis for works of love in
the Christian life; hence, they emphasized Christ as an example.

The second problem is highlighted by Fausto Sozzini, in his great
work *De Jesu Christo Servatore* (*On Jesus Christ as Savior*). Is it
moral for one person to die for another's sin? Is it appropriate for
me to sin and for Christ to die on my behalf? Is it appropriate for
God to deal with sinners in that kind of way? This is closely related
to another powerful criticism that Socinus makes of the classic penal
substitution theory of atonement: if Christ has died for your sins on
the cross, he has taken on the cross the punishment that your specific
sins deserve, and therefore God's forgiveness of you is not an act of
mercy. He has to let you off because the price has been paid.

Think about the force of this criticism. It can help if we draw
comparison with everyday life. If I default on my mortgage for the
next twelve months, let us say that, for some reason, my very wealthy
neighbor steps in and agrees to pay the bill for me. Then, when the
debt collectors turn up at my door, my neighbor comes around and
hands over the full amount of money I owe on my mortgage. In these
circumstances, it is not mercy for the debt collector to let me off. It
is not mercy for the debt collector not to seize my house. Given the
fact that the debt is paid, I have every legal right to retain possession
of my house at that point.

Socinus's deceptively simple, but nonetheless powerful, criticism
of penal substitution is this: if God has punished your sins on the

Lord Jesus Christ, you have a legal right to walk away unpunished and scot-free. That is not mercy. It is your right, a demand of justice, and Socinus would say that that does not square with the biblical teaching about God as both a just and a merciful God.

These are four basic criticisms that come to bear, four challenges that were raised, in the sixteenth and seventeenth centuries by Roman Catholicism, by Arminianism, by Amyraldianism, and by Socinianism. Each of these four problems is a hardy perennial in the Christian world. Catholicism raises the question of the once-and-for-all sufficiency of Christ's sacrifice. Arminianism and Amyraldianism raise the question of the connection between Christ's sacrifice and its efficacy for individual salvation. And Socinianism, in its rejection of penal substitution, resonates with many of the more recent challenges to orthodoxy on this point from within the evangelical community. Put simply, can God be just and merciful at the same time?

Hugo Grotius's Response to Socinus

Having seen these four challenges, we should also consider an early response to these matters, particularly to the Socinian challenge, as it is one of the more pungent critiques and, with the increasing abandonment of penal substitution in evangelical quarters, one of the more relevant to our own day.

Interestingly enough, one of the most powerful early responses to Socinus came not from Reformed Orthodox, although they were very interested and concerned about the issues involved, but from within the Arminian community in Holland. It came from the pen of one Hugo Grotius, a seventeenth-century Arminian theologian, one of the most brilliant men of his generation, a very clever theologian, extremely influential in the area of biblical exegesis and also, interestingly enough, one of the great legal theorists of the seventeenth century. Indeed, if you go to your local library or university library and type in the name Hugo Grotius, you are more likely to find books discussing Hugo Grotius's theory of law than those of his theology.

Hugo Grotius was very interested in matters of atonement, justice, and mercy. His theology and his legal interest overlap at this point. He developed and articulated what is often called the governmental theory of the atonement. This was the idea that man's sin represented a basic rebellion against God's sovereignty and against God's rule over this world; and thus it was important for God to make a point about who was in charge. He needed to make it clear to his creatures that he was in overall control, and by sacrificing his own Son on Calvary, he demonstrated how seriously he took sin, but he also showed that he was sovereign and was able to restore order over his creation. He did this, we might say, by showing that he took sin seriously by dealing with it, and by then moving on.

The significance of Grotius's critique of Socinianism lay in his borrowing of a distinction from the field of Roman law, an area where he was probably the greatest mind in his generation. In Latin the distinction is made between a *solutio eiusdem* and a *solutio tantidem*. A *solutio eiusdem* means a solution, a resolution, of the same thing. *Eiusdem* is Latin for "the same." A *solutio tantidem* means a solution or release of the equivalent, *tantidem* being Latin for "equivalent."

Consider again my illustration of defaulting on my mortgage. Having defaulted twelve months on my mortgage, let's say I owe 20,000 dollars to the mortgage company. The debt collector turns up at my door, and my neighbor comes over from his house; he asks what's going on; and I explain to him the situation. He pulls out his wallet, and he just happens to have twenty 1,000 dollar bills in his wallet. He hands them over to the debt collector, and it's all done. That's a *solutio eiusdem*. The identical thing that is required of me to resolve the debt has been handed over, and the debt collector is legally obliged to release me from the debt. He has no choice. He came to my house looking for 20,000 dollars. I hand him 20,000 dollars, and he is legally obliged to take it.

Now let's look at the same scenario but with a different resolution. Again, I've defaulted on my mortgage for twelve months, and a debt collector arrives at my door demanding 20,000 dollars. My next-door neighbor wanders over and asks what's going on. I explain the situation to him, and my neighbor points to the old but still reliable Alpha Romeo sports car on his drive, which, according to the Blue Book, happens to be worth 20,000 dollars. He says to the debt collector, "I don't have 20,000 dollars in my wallet, but what about my Alpha Romeo? The Blue Book says it's worth 20,000 dollars. Will you take that as an equivalent for the debt that's owed?" The debt collector thinks for a moment and says, "Yes, I think I can easily do that." He then takes the keys, starts the engine, drives off with 20,000 dollars of Alpha Romeo, and at the same time releases me from my debt. That's a *solutio tantidem*.

Notice the key difference here. In the first scenario, where my neighbor hands over 20,000 dollars on my behalf, the debt collector is legally obliged to take it and release me from my debt. There is no mercy in that situation; it is a simple matter of legal justice. In the second scenario, however, the debt collector is under no legal obligation to take the car, even though it's the precise equivalent of the 20,000-dollar debt. He does not need to take it, but he agrees to do so. In the second scenario, therefore, there is mercy as well as justice. The debt has been fully paid, but the debt collector had to make that critical decision out of the kindness of his heart that he was willing to accept the equivalent payment for the debt.

Now, transfer that idea to the cross of Calvary. Grotius says this is the answer to Socinus's challenge. The challenge, of course, was how sin could be really punished on the cross but God still be merciful. How does the sacrifice on Calvary have an objectivity that still allows room for God's mercy? Grotius says the mistake that so many of the Reformed have made is that they are operating with a model that says, for example, it is Trueman's sins, his actual sins, that are imputed to Christ on the cross of Calvary and are punished. Thus, if Trueman's sins have been punished on the cross of Calvary, then it is not mercy for God to forgive Trueman; it is justice. But,

Grotius says, if the punishment on the cross is merely an equivalent of Trueman's sins, then it is still possible to build mercy into the equation, for then God still has to make a *merciful* decision that he will accept this *equivalent* payment for Trueman's debt.

I am not a Grotian on the atonement, but I have to say that this is one of those arguments that is so beautifully worked out that you can't help but stand back and admire it. He sees the power of the theological critique being offered, and he responds in a way that is subtle and precise and deals in a most wonderful way with the issue.

There are many theological problems with Grotius's response to Socinianism, most of which are too extensive for this brief treatment. Central, however, is this: if Trueman's sins are not imputed to Christ, then it's arguable that Christ's righteousness is not imputed to Trueman. That fits well with an Arminian understanding of justification, but I can assure you that Trueman has a problem with understanding that Christ's righteousness is not imputed to him. So this is one major theological problem generated by Grotius, in this case relative to the Adam/Christ parallel in Romans 5.

John Owen and Richard Baxter

Writing as a historian, I think perhaps the best way to conclude this study of post-Reformation atonement developments is to turn to biography. In the post-Reformation scene in England, two powerful and important figures, John Owen and Richard Baxter, will highlight the state of affairs. Let's look first at John Owen and then Richard Baxter and then finally return to John Owen.

John Owen's most famous work is titled *The Death of Death in the Death of Christ* (1647). Owen (1616–1683) was just thirty-one years old when he wrote this book. He was not of dissimilar age to many theological students today. If I were to use this book as the basic criteria of how I mark essays in my classes, it would go very badly with most of the students, since Owen's book shows a mastery not only of the biblical text but of logic, philosophy, and historic

Christian texts as well. It is famous (or infamous) as the most elaborate and profound articulation of limited atonement ever written. In fact, the book is not so much about the question of limited atonement as it is about the closely related issue of the efficaciousness of Christ's death. Owen was worried about the Roman Catholic and Arminian challenges that separate Christ's death from its efficacy, and if you have a view of Christ's death that ties in closely to its efficacy, you are inevitably going to end up with something looking like what we now call limited atonement or particular redemption.

Owen on the Atonement

How did Owen work out his argument? First, critical to Owen was the relationship between the New Testament and the Old Testament. Owen saw a profound connection between the Old Testament priesthood and Christ's priestly action in the New Testament. This alone prevented him from going down the Amyraldian route that drives a wedge between Christ's death on the cross and his intercession at the right hand of the Father. Owen argued that in the Old Testament the sacrifice of the animal and the pouring out of the blood of the animal as an offering on the altar are two sides of the same coin. The animal is not sacrificed for one group of people while the blood is poured out only for some subset of that group. In other words, the slaughter of the sacrifice and the offering up of the sacrifice are for the same restricted group of people, ancient Israel.

Owen saw that unity of sacrificial action in the Old Testament as being the background against which one must read the unity of the sacrificial action of Christ in the New Testament. Christ is sacrificed and poured out, dies and intercedes, for one and the same group of people. There is a unity between the cross of Calvary and the right hand of God the Father that must be maintained in fidelity to Old Testament types.

It is important to make this point at the start, because there are many who see limited atonement as a mere logical deduction from the doctrine of election and reprobation. That is far too simplistic a way of looking at it, because there is considerable exegesis underlying the notion of limited atonement and a great deal of sophisticated reflection upon the connections between Old Testament and New Testament in the development of the concept. Thus, to disagree with limited atonement you must disagree with the exegesis that underlies it and reject the understanding of the relationship between Old Testament types and New Testament antitypes. You should not dismiss limited atonement as a naïve, overly logical deduction from doctrine of election, because that simply is not the case, as is demonstrated by Owen's text.

Secondly, for Owen the death of Christ needs to be understood in the context of Adam and the covenant of works. Incidentally, Owen saw the covenant of works as being rooted in Romans 5, not explicitly in Genesis 1 to 3. There are those who ask where the covenant is mentioned in the early chapters of Genesis. It isn't mentioned in the early chapters of Genesis! But, historically, Reformed Orthodoxy came to apply the notion of covenant to the early chapters of Genesis on the basis of the Adam/Christ parallel in Romans 5. Adam is seen to be determinative of humanity's problem, as he is a representative of the whole of humanity, a role which Orthodox Reformed scholars articulated by using the language of covenant, a relationship involving two parties with conditions and rewards attached. When Adam falls, God's justice is offended by Adam's sin and sacrifice is required as a propitiation.

This is where the connection between Adam and Christ is established: Christ's work, under the new covenant, is designed to achieve what Adam could not and to deal with the problem that his fall created. There is thus a clear connection between Adam and Christ and between the Old Testament priesthood and Christ's priestly action. Adam is representative. Christ is representative. The covenant of works determined the nature of Adam's obligation and the extent of his fall. The new covenant determined the nature of

Christ's work. As Adam represented more than himself, so Christ will represent more than himself.

In this context, Owen thought it very important to argue that the sins of the elect are imputed to Christ, so Christ actually shoulders our sins as he is sacrificed. Thus, for Owen, the Grotian distinction between *solutio eiusdem* and *solutio tantidem*, between the same thing and an equivalent thing, is not an option. Owen, of course, was aware of the Socinian critique, but he argued that the mercy of God's action lies in the fact that God never had to take his action in the first place. God could have simply punished us all in hell. Instead, he decided to do something he did not have to do. He decided to send his own Son to die for us, and it is this action and decision that grounds mercy for the Protestant understanding of atonement. It is, if you like, God's free and gracious decision to move in the direction of salvation that establishes mercy.

Baxter on the Atonement

Let us now think about Richard Baxter, who was a year older than Owen (b. 1615). Baxter probably wrote more words in the English language than any person who has ever lived. His wife made the famous comment that if he had thought more and written less, he would have been of far more use to the church. Baxter is significant for our purposes because it was his criticisms of Owen that sharpened Owen's own thinking on atonement.

To understand Baxter on atonement, you need to understand something from his background. Richard Baxter cut his teeth as a chaplain in the army in the English Civil War. What Baxter experienced in the Parliamentary Army in the English Civil War was rampant sectarianism and chaos. He interpreted this theologically, as the Protestant doctrine of justification by faith being used as an excuse for chaos and license.

If he was nothing else, Baxter was a man who loved order and hierarchy. Take, for example, some advice in his very famous book

The Reformed Pastor, the book that Spurgeon used to have his wife read to him every Sunday evening. Here Baxter makes the comment that every time a preacher preaches, he must make sure that he says one thing that nobody in the congregation understands. What is the reason for such a strange piece of advice? Baxter answers that if the congregation understands everything the pastor says, it will lead to chaos: the people will think they can do the pastor's job, kick him out, and just take over. You need to maintain the hierarchy by preaching at least one incomprehensible point every Sunday. (Would that most preachers say only one thing that is incomprehensible!)

This gives an idea of Baxter and his outlook. Here is someone who feared anarchy and chaos, and who felt the power of the Socinian critique. Indeed, he felt the power of the Socinian critique of Reformed Orthodoxy at this point: if the sins of the elect, the sins of believers, are really imputed to Christ and are dealt with in him, then, when he dies on Calvary, those sins are immediately forgiven. In other words, Baxter sees the classic Reformed understanding of atonement as in some way demanding the doctrine of eternal justification whereby the elect are always justified from the moment of birth, and that faith does not involve a movement from wrath to grace in history but, rather, the realization that you are that which you always have been—forgiven of your sins.

Thus, as Baxter witnessed the chaos of England in the 1640s, he thought that he was seeing the ill effects of Reformed Orthodoxy being worked out all around him as the Sectarians and the Antinomians went on an amoral rampage. He also felt that the Reformed doctrine of the atonement gave him nothing to work with to maintain the order and hierarchy that he felt should mark a Christian society. So Baxter attacked Owen on this very point: if Christ really has our sins imputed to him on the cross, why is it that we are not immediately forgiven? And to solve this dilemma, Baxter adopted the Grotian distinction between Christ's death as equivalent for our sins and Christ's death being a like substitute. He further argued that it is by faith and by walking obediently that we ultimately receive the benefit of Christ's death. So Baxter maintained a place for both faith and good works in justification by driving a wedge between our actual sins and that which is punished on Christ at Calvary.

Owen's Response to Baxter

Now let us glance briefly at Owen's response to Baxter. Owen certainly felt the force of Baxter's critique. Yet Owen maintained, and argued exegetically, that there must be a real imputation of our actual sins to Christ. He also came to accent the instrumentality of faith in uniting us to Christ. Owen did not see the problem that Baxter raised about our sins being punished on the cross of Calvary, relative to the idea of eternal justification.

At one point Owen answered this with a rather weak analogy, saying that forgiveness is a bit like a man lying in prison in York and being pardoned in London; thus, somebody has to ride from London to York to tell him the good news, and it takes three or four days to get there before he can hand over the pardon. So legally speaking the man in prison is actually pardoned from the moment the pardon is signed, but he is still in prison until the prison guard gets the news. The weakness of this analogy is that it still looks a bit like eternal justification. We can say that, legally speaking, he is really forgiven even if, experientially, he is still languishing in prison.

Owen does not want to concede that point, because he wants to maintain the real movement from wrath to grace in history. So what Owen does is emphasize union with Christ at this point. Faith unites a believer to Christ, and it is only in the context of this union with Christ that his righteousness is imputed to us. In short, he comes to accent what I call the historical economy in a much sharper way than he did earlier.

Owen's fear of Socinianism also led him to make an important shift in his understanding of God's attributes. In 1647 Owen argued that, had God so willed it, he could have just forgiven humanity's sin by a mere act of will. By 1652, however, he was arguing that if God chooses to save, he has to become incarnate to do it because, once God has made the decision to save, there is an absolute necessity according to his essential justice for God to become incarnate and die on the cross of Calvary for the forgiveness of sin. In this, Owen clearly wanted to avoid any way of making it appear that Christ's atonement is at all unnecessary.

This is reminiscent of the words of H. R. Macintosh, the twentieth-century theologian who went so far as to say that as soon as you start arguing that Christ's atonement is not, strictly speaking, absolutely necessary for salvation, but only on the basis of an arbitrary act of God's will, you are halfway to denying the atonement as a whole.

Controversy and Progress

It has been said that the Reformed Orthodox were so concerned about Socinianism after the sixteenth century that it drove them to narrow their discussions of atonement in a way that undermined some of the richness of biblical teaching on Christ's atonement. I would argue the contrary on the basis of what we have seen, particularly in John Owen and his engagement with the Socinians and Richard Baxter. Even in this narrow and superficial survey, we find profound reflection upon the relationship between the Old Testament and the New and between Adam and Christ relative to Christ's atonement.

We also see the emergence of an obvious connection between atonement and justification. We see an acute awareness in the way that all this must be worked out in relation to the moral imperatives of the Christian life. And we see considerable and detailed reflection upon the notion of mercy, and how mercy and justice connect together in God. If we were to dig deeper, we would also see that Orthodox Reformed theologians, in their reflections on atonement, have much to say about Christology and Trinitarianism, which helps further to integrate Protestant insights with the wider catholic legacy of creedal Christianity.

I noted at the beginning of this chapter that the Reformation makes it clear that the atonement is extremely important for the everyday pastoral work of the church, and you see this reflected in the sophisticated discussions between Baxter and Owen. How does the atonement connect to good works and moral imperatives? We do not see a repudiation of the Reformation or the Reformation concerns, or even a particular narrowing of focus. We see, rather, an increasing depth of theological discussion and pastoral connection relating to the atonement and subsequent issues.

Discussion of these matters continues today. Perhaps the most relevant lesson for us from post-Reformation developments on the atonement is our need to recognize the interconnectedness of atonement theology with every other locus of Christian faith. Are we being careful to understand the implications of our thinking on the person of Christ, on the nature of God, on the continuity between the Old Testament and the New Testament in such vital matters as the priesthood of Christ, and the link between the atonement and Christian assurance?

If we will emulate the best of post-Reformation theologians, we will dedicate ourselves to the kind of scholarship that reflects deeply on exegetical issues, that is, biblical theology, in tandem with the inter-relatedness of all Christian teaching within the completed canon, that is, systematic theology. To do anything less than to hold these together, thinking deeply and carefully, we will fail to leave the kind of legacy left by the Reformed scholars of the sixteenth and seventeenth centuries, but instead will leave behind us a trail of false leads and muddled thinking that is unworthy of so sublime a topic as the atoning work of our Lord.

PENAL SUBSTITUTIONARY ATONEMENT AND ITS "NON-VIOLENT" CRITICS

Richard D. Phillips

Like countless other evangelical parents, my wife and I have sat down with our children to tell them about the saving blood of Jesus: "We want you to know that we are all sinners, guilty under God's law and deserving his just condemnation. But the good news is that God sent his Son, Jesus, to bear the penalty for our sins by dying for us. We are forgiven by trusting that Jesus died in our place on the cross."

Voices against the Atonement

Any moderately informed Christian realizes that those words about salvation are deeply offensive to many people. First, we have called everyone sinners, deserving the judgment of hell. Furthermore, we say that men and women can be accepted by God only through what theologians call penal substitutionary atonement: Christ died as our substitute, receiving from the just God the penalty our sins deserve. Christians know that people who think themselves good and deserving of God's praise do not appreciate this message. A better informed evangelical will also realize that many professing Christians, namely, adherents of liberal theology, also find this offensive. It was really no scandal, therefore, when the secular humanist and Episcopal bishop John Shelby Spong wrote of the cross: "I would choose to loathe rather than to worship a deity who required the sacrifice of his son."[1]

What few cross-loving Christians realize is that a surprising number of scholars who consider themselves evangelicals, and who are received as such by evangelical institutions, now speak in equally violent terms against the idea that Jesus died to pay for our sins. Probably the most notorious example comes from British evangelical Steve Chalke's popular book *The Lost Message of Jesus*, in which he describes the classic evangelical doctrine of the atonement as "a form of cosmic child abuse—a vengeful Father, punishing his Son for an offence he has not even committed."[2]

Some might be inclined to write this off as an isolated eccentricity, but the briefest examination will reveal an iceberg under this sharply pointed barb. Joel B. Green and Mark D. Baker wrote that in the traditional evangelical doctrine of the cross "God takes on the role of the sadist inflicting punishment, while Jesus, in his role as masochist, readily embraces suffering."[3] Michael Hardin writes of receiving an evangelical mass mailing just days after a recent tragedy in which a number of Amish school children were savagely murdered. The flier invited people to church, where they would hear that on the cross God punished Jesus for our sins: "Jesus took the place of sinners," the church mailing read. Hardin sees a direct parallel between the God of this gospel and the angry gunman in the Amish schoolhouse. Reportedly, the gunman acted out of anger for the death of his own daughter some years earlier; police overheard him telling his victims, "I'm going to make you pay for my daughter." Hardin writes: "The atonement sought by the shooter . . . is no different than that sought by the God of the mailing. For both, blood satisfies, and in both, innocent blood, truly innocent blood is shed."[4] All of these quotes are found in books from publishing houses long identified with evangelical Christianity.

It turns out that while Christians in the pews are lustily singing about the blood of Jesus, a violent assault is being launched from within evangelical academia against the chief claim on which our hope rests. Hardin accurately notes: "In the last decade the overwhelming majority of books published on the atonement, in one way or another, revise, critique, dismiss or outright reject the penal satisfaction theory of the atonement."[5]

The purpose of this chapter, therefore, is to take note of the objections leveled against penal substitutionary atonement, to isolate the central issues, and finally to offer a biblical defense of this doctrine, which J. I. Packer described only thirty-five years ago as a key "distinguishing mark of the worldwide evangelical fraternity, namely, the belief that Christ's death on the cross had the character of *penal substitution*, and that it was in virtue of this fact that it brought salvation to mankind."[6]

Penal Substitution and Its Evangelical Critics

It is no surprise that the doctrine of atonement requires the qualification of add-on labels. As Philip Ryken pointed out earlier in this book, the word *atonement* was invented by William Tyndale for his English Bible to convey the "at-one-ment" resulting from Christ's death on the cross.[7] The question necessarily follows as to *how* Christ reconciled us to God, and specifically what it was about Christ's death that makes sinners at one with God. For this reason, any full treatment of the doctrine of atonement requires a lengthier formula.

The conviction expressed in this book is that sinners are reconciled to God by means of Christ's *penal, substitutionary atonement*. This means that the central truth about the cross is that Jesus died as the substitute for sinners before God—suffering vicariously in our place and as our representative—and that he died to suffer the wrath of God that we deserve and to pay the penalty for our sins under the divine justice of God's law. We acknowledge that there are other models that helpfully work out other aspects of the atonement, such as the *Christus Victor* view that emphasizes the cross as Christ's cosmic victory over the powers of evil, and the therapeutic view that emphasizes the healing brought through Christ's self-sacrificial death. But, in company with classic Reformed and evangelical theology since the Reformation, we hold to penal substitution as the central and controlling model for understanding the biblical revelation of the cross.

In many of the scholarly books recently published on the atonement, you will find a multifaceted approach strongly espoused. For instance, Joel Green and Mark Baker argue, "The idea that the Bible or the classical Christian tradition has 'one' view of the atonement is unfounded," citing "constellations of images" in the Bible to unpack so great a mystery as the atoning death of God's Son.[8] Yet the urgent theme of this and other recent studies of the atonement is not merely the urge to include various strands of insight regarding the cross, but a violent determination to exclude one particular theory of atonement, namely, penal substitutionary atonement.

Using Green and Baker as a typical example, we see that while they favor "constellations of images," their chief object is to see the eclipse of penal substitution. Arguing that this doctrine involves a misuse of Scripture, that it reflects the values of a bygone medieval Western culture obsessed with guilt and justice, and that it poorly represents Christianity in a postmodern world more interested in relationships than in authority, they conclude their book-long polemic by asserting: "We believe that the popular fascination with and commitment to penal substitutionary atonement has had ill effects in the life of the church in the United States and has little to offer the global church and mission by way of understanding or embodying the message of Jesus Christ."[9]

In fact, such recent academic studies of the atonement do not have the purpose merely of promoting a truly multifaceted approach to the atonement but, rather, the replacement of penal substitutionary atonement with a different approach that emphasizes the centrality of non-violence in the atoning work of Christ. While all must admit the violence of man at the cross, these theologians contest any idea that God achieved salvation by his own plan or participation in Jesus' bloody death.

At the heart of this movement is a rejection of the idea of God's wrath, a repudiation of divine retributive justice, gross offense at the idea that God would punish his innocent Son for our sins, and a conviction that the traditional evangelical view of the cross is in conflict with Jesus' teaching of non-violence and is thus responsible for fostering a culture of violence, abuse, and victimhood. Joan Carlson Brown and Rebecca Parker express the general conviction of those opposed to penal substitution: "Until this image is shattered it will be almost impossible to create a just society."[10] While the case against a "violent" atonement includes a blizzard of criticisms, the above noted objections are most significant.

The first is a complaint about the emphasis given to *God's wrath* under penal substitution. Brad Jersak asserts, "The atonement is non-penal. Good Friday was not the outpouring of God's violence upon Christ to assuage his own wrath. That day was God's 'No!' to wrath and 'Yes!' to love and forgiveness in the face of *our* violence and wrath."[11] Green and Baker summarize: "The Scriptures as a whole provide no ground for a portrait of an angry God needing to be appeased in atoning sacrifice."[12] Therefore, they complain that penal substitution presents "a God from whom we need to be saved!"[13]

A second, and related, complaint against penal substitution is that it assumes a God who responds to sin with *retributive justice.* Jersak writes that "the picture of God derived from penal substitution looks vindictive and untrustworthy, repulsed by sinners and rather different from the Father's heart as portrayed perfectly by Jesus."[14] Or, as Gregory Boyd puts it in highly charged language: "How is the view that God requires a kill to have his rage placated essentially

different from the pagan or magical understanding of divine appease-
ment found in primordial religions?"[15]

This is all the more a problem to such critics when it comes to
a third issue, the idea of God punishing his innocent Son for sins he
did not commit. Apart from the apparent injustice attributed to penal
substitution, the problem is raised that "it presumes *a breakdown
of the inner-trinitarian life of God.*"[16] That God would set forth his
own Son to be the substitute who bears our sin is considered morally
dubious, as well as an affront to the Bible's teaching of God's love
for his only-begotten.

Arising out of this supposedly twisted morality is an ethic that
justifies violence among our fellow men and promotes submissive
victimhood. Thus Sharon Baker writes, "Lurking behind [penal sub-
stitute] theories is the ghost of a punitive father, haunting the image
of forgiving grace by finding the death of his own son an agreeable
way to negotiate forgiving the world." With this image in mind, she
suggests, "traditional atonement theory lends legitimacy to social
and personal violence."[17]

Lastly, those advocating a non-violent theory of the atonement
assert that under the penal substitution theory, God is made to *violate
his own ethics of peace and love* as taught by Jesus. Steve Chalke
argues: "If the cross is a personal act of violence perpetrated by God
towards humankind but borne by his Son, then it makes a mockery
of Jesus' own teaching to love your enemies and to refuse to repay
evil with evil."[18]

While authors espousing a non-violent atonement offer a variety of ways to understand the mechanisms of its working, they are
united in the quest to strip from the cross any idea that God himself
was punishing sin in the person of his Son. Michael Hardin waxes
optimistic about this new awareness of divine non-violence in the
cross: "Christianity stands on the verge of trusting a God who is love
alone and not a mixed God, a Christian version of divine schizo-
phrenia."[19] This is conceived as the greatest need of our war-torn

world, given that our image of God determines our moral choices. The bottom line of this quest for non-violence is summed up by J. Denny Weaver: "Anyone uncomfortable with the idea of a God who sanctions violence, a God who sends the Son so that his death can satisfy a divine requirement, should abandon satisfaction and Anselmian atonement forthwith."[20]

Assessing the Issues

But what does the Bible say? Christians committed to a robust doctrine of biblical authority will want to construct their beliefs not out of the cloth of their own comforts but out of the loom of God's revealed Word. Having identified these four key complaints leveled against the classic evangelical doctrine of penal substitutionary atonement, I will respond to these four criticisms as a way of unfolding the Bible's teaching on Christ's atoning death. Denny Weaver refers to all four of these topics in his complaint: "Satisfaction depends on a divinely sanctioned death as that which is necessary to satisfy the offended divine entity, whether God or God's law or God's honor. Satisfaction atonement depends on the assumption that doing justice means to punish, that a wrong deed is balanced by violence."[21] So which assumptions are valid, and what does the Bible say?

Divine Wrath?

The first question to ask pertains to the nature and character of God. Does the Bible emphasize God's wrath in responding to sin? If the Bible does, how are we to understand God's wrath biblically?

It is true that God's wrath may be presented in unbalanced ways, as is frequently pointed out in the critical literature, but as to the question of God's wrath itself, the Bible leaves no honest room for doubt. Starting with the Old Testament, I. Howard Marshall comments "that references to God's anger . . . can be counted in their hundreds."[22] Thus Isaiah 51:22 speaks candidly about Israel having been forced to drink from the "cup" or "bowl" of God's wrath.

In Hosea 8:5, God says of the idols of Samaria, "My anger burns against them"; that exact language is used in Job 42:7 when the Lord denounces Job's false-speaking friends.

But this language is not restricted to the Old Testament, lest we think that the coming of Christ has softened God's fury against evil. The apostle Paul famously declares that "the wrath of God is revealed from heaven against all ungodliness and unrighteousness of men, who by their unrighteousness suppress the truth" (Rom. 1:18). No amount of dissembling on this clear and important statement, such as Green and Baker's facile argument that Paul is not referring to actual wicked acts but only a God-denying disposition,[23] can blunt the clear force of Paul's teaching regarding God's personal anger toward men for their sinful deeds (e.g., see Rom. 2:4–5). Nor can it fairly be argued that God's wrath, such as it is, consists only of his giving over of sinful men to the natural consequences of their actions, as it widely argued by non-violent atonement theologians. When this argument was floated early in the twentieth century, R. V. G. Tasker accurately replied: "[God's wrath] is rather a personal quality, without which God would cease to be fully righteous and his love would degenerate into sentimentality."[24]

This personal quality in God's wrath is seen especially in the book of Revelation. Consider the plight of those who worship the Beast, who as a result "will drink the wine of God's wrath, poured full strength into the cup of his anger" (Rev. 14:10). The intentional and active role given to God's wrath is illustrated by God's command in the judgment of Babylon the Great (Rev. 16:19), "to make her drain the cup of the wine of the fury of his wrath." Observe that it is God who "makes" his enemies to drain the cup of "his wrath." Similarly definitive is the image of the reigning and victorious Christ, who is "clothed in a robe dipped in blood" and who "will tread the winepress of the fury of the wrath of God the Almighty" (Rev. 19:13, 15). This is the farthest thing from the pacifist, sentimental deity of the non-violent theologians, who regrets that sin carries within itself its own punishment.

Jesus gave the same witness to God's wrath. For instance, in a parable comparing God to a merciful master who is angered by the hard-heartedness of his servant, Jesus said, "In anger his master delivered him to the jailers, until he should pay all his debt" (Matt. 18:34). Against the backdrop of the vast biblical witness to God's personal wrath against sin and sinners, John Stott could scarcely be charged of exaggeration when he wrote: "The essential background to the cross is not only the sin, responsibility and guilt of human beings but the just reaction of God to these things, in other words his holiness and wrath."[25]

It is true, of course, that divine wrath must be understood as it is presented in the Scriptures and not as imagined by the fantasies of men. We must therefore realize that God's anger at sin is not an uncontrolled rage. Stott explains: "God's anger is absolutely pure and uncontaminated by those elements which render human anger sinful. . . . No nightmare of an indiscriminate, uncontrolled, irrational fury, but the wrath of the holy and merciful God called forth by, and directed against, men's *asebeia* (ungodliness) and *adikia* (unrighteousness)."[26] Instead, Stott writes, "The wrath of God . . . is his steady, unrelenting, unremitting, uncompromising antagonism to evil in all its forms and manifestations."[27]

Moreover, it is not obvious why the feeling of wrath should be inappropriate to God. I. Howard Marshall comments, "If God feels other emotions, such as tender compassion, it is difficult to see why he should not feel some kind of revulsion against evil." In reality, Marshall continues, "To deny that God feels some kind of negative feeling about sin seems to be a denial of the personal character of God who reacts to the evil that ruins his creation and destroys his relationship with his creatures. It is to make the judgment something impersonal and mechanistic rather than the personal reaction of the living God."[28]

Indeed, far from God's wrath casting doubt upon his moral perfection, it is necessary to it. In a justly famous paragraph, J. I. Packer
answers objections to the morality of divine wrath:

> This is *righteous* anger—the *right* reaction of moral perfection in
> the Creator towards moral perversity in the creature. So far from
> the manifestation of God's wrath in punishing sin being morally
> doubtful, the thing that would be morally doubtful would be for
> Him *not* to show His wrath in this way. God is not *just*—that is,
> He does not act in the way that is *right*, He does not do what is
> proper to a *judge*—unless He inflicts upon all sin and wrongdoing
> the penalty it deserves.[29]

This reminds us that all of God's attributes are perfectly joined to
the others, and all of God's actions reflect all of his personal perfections.
God's wrath in Christ's penal, substitutionary atonement is especially
an expression of God's holiness in demanding satisfaction and of God's
righteousness in an act of judgment for the sins of Christ's people. But
just as God's holiness is inseparable from his other attributes, we must
say that his wrath is a loving wrath, a faithful wrath, a just wrath, and
for those who will stand before him on the day of judgment without
the benefit of Christ's atoning blood, it will be an eternal wrath.

Retributive Justice?

Closely related to the complaint against the traditional understanding of God's wrath is the criticism of God's judgment as retributive
justice. Stephen Travis has written that "the judgment of God is to
be seen not primarily in terms of retribution, whereby people are
'paid back' according to their deeds, but in terms of non-relationship
to Christ."[30] Moreover, the non-violent atonement view generally
argues that to the extent that sin is punished, this judgment occurs
simply due to the natural processes of sin.

Responding to these arguments, Garry J. Williams points out that
even if judgment is intrinsic to sin due to the workings of this world,

it was God who designed and made the world in which sin carries its own judgment. Indeed, it is clearly the case that sin does carry its own judgment, and it does so because God has willed this for his creation. Williams thus argues, "The kind of process described in the Proverbs in which someone digs a hole and falls into it can, when the process is created and sustained by God, still be understood as retributive."[31] Williams made this argument specifically to counter the assumption made by Stephen Travis and others that judgment is only retributive when it is "outside" of the process, as a deliberate intervention from the normal course of events by God (an assumption used by Travis to adapt biblical material to his non-retributive thesis).

Yet it must be further observed that a great amount of biblical material depicts divine judgment in a way that is not intrinsic to sin. In other words, God's judgment often takes the form of deliberate interventions on God's part that are beyond the normal course of sin bringing misery and ruin. Williams cites as an example God's plagues on Pharaoh and Egypt in the book of Exodus: "The era of the exodus was not just a good time for frogs, gnats, flies and locusts, let alone for the death of firstborn children."[32] The same might be said for Noah's flood, the slaying of Ananias and Sapphira (Acts 5:9), and the fall of Jerusalem to the siege engines of Nebuchadnezzar, the latter of which was a long-prophesied event in divine retribution for Israel's covenant-breaking sins (see Isa. 29:1–8; Jer. 37:6–10; Mic. 3:12).

Consider God's judgment on Achan for the sin of violating God's command to take no spoils from the conquest of Jericho. Not only was this judgment not merely the natural outworking of Achan's sin, but without God's direct revelation no one would even have learned about the stash of gold, silver, and precious cloths hidden beneath Achan's tent. God responded to the sin of this one man by causing the nation to lose an important battle, with considerable loss of life (Josh. 7:1–5).

It is impossible to see how this national defeat was the natural, intrinsic outworking of Achan's theft; indeed, the Bible specifies that

this resulted because of God's anger for Achan's sin (Josh. 7:1).
God's wrath was then directed specifically at Achan himself, and the
nature of this judgment can only be described as retributive justice.
Achan was brought to the Valley of Achor, along with his stolen
objects, together with his sons and daughters and all his household
possessions: "And all Israel stoned him with stones. They burned
them with fire and stoned them with stones. And they raised over
him a great heap of stones that remains to this day. Then the LORD
turned from his burning anger" (Josh. 7:25–26). There simply is no
other description for God's response to Achan's sin but divine wrath
pouring out in retributive justice. In Travis's terms, Achan clearly
was "paid back" by God according to his sinful deeds.

So also will it be, according to the Bible, when Christ returns
to judge the world. Williams writes: "On the last day, Jesus Christ
will intervene in history as judge. He will stop the progress of world
history, raise the dead and pronounce judgment on them. Left to
itself, this would not happen to the world."[33] The final judgment
being the ultimate expression of God's judgment, and the danger for
which the atoning death of Christ is God's remedy, we must conclude that retributive justice is not merely an acceptable definition
of God's judgment but the primary and controlling understanding
for that judgment that is threatened against sinful mankind by Holy
Scripture.

What, then, of the complaints raised against retributive justice?
Non-violent atonement theorists complain that in the traditional
understanding of divine wrath and retributive justice, God is the One
from whom we must be saved. Biblically considered, this statement
must be reverently affirmed. The chief and ultimate threat against
sinful mankind is indeed God himself—the holy, righteous, and just
God who must and will personally judge sin with retributive justice
by pouring out the bowls of his holy wrath. It is from the judgment
of his own wrath that God graciously provides salvation through
faith in Jesus Christ. Of this, the writer of Hebrews asks, "How

shall we escape if we neglect such a great salvation?" (Heb. 2:3), and further declares, "It is a fearful thing to fall into the hands of the living God" (Heb. 10:31).

An Affront to Inner-Trinitarian Love?

But how could God have purposed and acted to harm, and even kill, his own Son, given the Bible's teaching of the perfect love within the relationships of the Trinity? How could the Father have punished Jesus, with whom, God insists, he is "well pleased" (Matt. 3:17)? And what kind of God, the non-violent atonement rhetoric fumes, would so violently punish his *innocent* Son? Taken together, these questions compose a third objection to penal substitution, complaining that it necessitates an unthinkable violation of the inner-Trinitarian love depicted in Scripture.

An initial answer is to call for less heated forms of expression. None but the most unguarded and reckless exponent of penal substitution would suggest that God the Father was punishing Jesus on the cross, as if God's Son had done something wrong or offensive. When traditional evangelical teachers of the cross point to passages such as Zechariah 13:7: "'Awake, O sword, against my shepherd,' . . . declares the LORD," and Isaiah 53:10: "It was the will of the LORD to crush him" as foretelling Christ's atoning death, we do not understand God as inflicting judgment on *Christ*, but judgment on *our sins*, which Christ bore. As Isaiah foretold, Christ was "stricken for the transgression of [God's] people" (Isa. 53:8).

Instead, a more responsible understanding of penal substitutionary atonement will make careful distinctions regarding the subject and object of the atonement. Christ is not the *object* of God's punishment on the cross, any more than God the Father is the object of Christ's persuasion in securing our forgiveness. Instead, in the most meaningful sense, God the Father and God the Son were both the *subjects* of the cross: that is, the atonement was an act they purposed and accomplished together.

So it is with the whole compass of Christ's redemptive work: "For I have come down from heaven, not to do my own will but the will of him who sent me" (John 6:38), he said. Jesus insisted that he would lay down his life "of my own accord" (John 10:18). Paul taught that Jesus "gave himself for me" (Gal. 2:20). On the cross, justice was served on the sins of God's people, by an act of atonement that was purposed, willed, and achieved by the cojoined persons of the Trinity.

Indeed, not only does penal substitution not offend the biblical doctrine of the Trinity, but it relies upon it. Garry Williams writes: "The reason that no conscious advocate of penal substitution thinks of the Son simply as the object of the Father's action is that the doctrine has been formed within a conscious, mature doctrine of the Trinity. Penal substitution in fact relies on a careful grounding in Augustine's principle that since the Father, the Son and the Holy Spirit are inseparable, so they work inseparably."[34]

In fact, understanding the Trinity properly, we also realize that to the extent that we may refer to Christ as the object of the atonement, he was not the sole object. For by the principle of the co-inhering of the persons of the Trinity, it was God who suffered for our sins, including God the Father and God the Spirit along with God the Son. Indeed, it is only by profound ignorance or neglect of the doctrine of the Trinity that evangelicals can join their voices to the blasphemous charge against the atonement, long trumpeted by liberal critics, of "cosmic child abuse."

To the extent that one might consider Christ the object of the atonement, and we must affirm the Scripture that describes him as "smitten by God" (Isa. 53:4), Christ was a most willing object. Yet he was also the subject of the atonement: it was his work that was done. Moreover, the Father who is accused of abusing his Son was in fact suffering the cross through his perfect ontological unity with the Son. Here we see the age-old problem with human analogies for inner-Trinitarian relations, especially when those analogies are used to heap such scorn on the character of God as to compare it to human child abuse.

With the Trinity properly accounted for in the atonement, we must realize that the Bible not only insists that God did lay the punishment of our sins upon the back of his perfectly beloved Son, but moreover that it "pleased" God to do this. It is with this language that the Authorized Version correctly renders Isaiah 53:10: "Yet it pleased the LORD to bruise him." It leaves one practically speechless to read how professing Christians place on this the character of sadism. These precious words direct our minds to the deepest mystery of the unfathomable purpose of God's matchless love: that the triune God would be pleased to be both subject and object of his own wrath, all so that unworthy sinners might be delivered from the just punishment of our sins against him. That the Scripture uses such language merely confronts us with our utter inability to sit in judgment on the character and morality of God, whose ways in grace are as high above our reckoning as the heavens are above the earth (cf. Isa. 55:8–9).

Conflict with Jesus' Ethical Teaching?

Lastly, we must confront the criticism that the violence of penal substitution utterly conflicts with the morality taught by Jesus himself. Does God's violent wrath toward sinners, and even more so toward his innocent Son, make, as Steve Chalke says, "a mockery of Jesus' own teaching to love your enemies and to refuse to repay evil with evil"?[35] Furthermore, if God forgives sin because his justice has been served at the cross, then is it true that he cannot be considered a God of grace but only one of strict justice?

The best, and most obvious, reply to the question of the atonement and Christian ethics is given by J. I. Packer, who identifies this as "a 'naturalistic' criticism, which assumes that what man could not do or would not require, God will not do or require either. Such criticism is profoundly perverse, for it shrinks God the Creator into the image of man the creature." Citing just one example of the evident biblical difference between human ethics and the divine economy, Packer notes that for a human to justify the guilty is perfidy, whereas for God to justify sinners is grace.[36]

When we consult the Bible, we find that the basis for Christian ethics is, in fact, the righteousness of God both in judgment and salvation. Thus the apostle Paul insists that Christians must not take revenge on their enemies. Does Paul give as his reason that God himself would never take vengeance and therefore his people must not as well? Not at all. In fact, it is precisely because of God's vengeance that Christians are not to seek revenge: "Beloved, never avenge yourselves, but leave it to the wrath of God, for it is written, 'Vengeance is mine, I will repay, says the Lord'" (Rom. 12:19).

Garry Williams thus observes, "Where [critics of penal substitution] would have us infer that God would never do what he tells us not to do, Paul argues the very opposite. God would have us not do what he does precisely because he does it. God says, 'do as I say, not as I do,' and justly so, since he is God and we are not."[37]

What of the argument that penal substitution undercuts God's mercy and love in salvation, since the atonement is so careful to fulfill God's justice? The answer is that this objection flies in the face of the Bible's most clear statements regarding God's motives in the cross. Paul insists that "God shows his love for us in that while we were still sinners, Christ died for us" (Rom. 5:8).

So clearly does the apostle John see the connection between God's merciful love and the atonement that he literally cannot speak of the former without the latter. For John, penal substitutionary atonement is *the* display of God's love: "In this is love, not that we have loved God but that he loved us and sent his Son to be the propitiation for our sins" (1 John 4:10). I. Howard Marshall explains: "The motive for the death of Jesus is stated to be the loving purpose of God, and there is not the faintest hint in the New Testament that Jesus died to persuade God to forgive sinners. On the contrary, his death is part of the way in which God himself acts in his mercy and grace."[38]

This observation prompts two reminders. On the one hand, we must always remember that the cross displays more than the glory of God's mercy and love, for Christ's death also shows forth God's holiness and righteousness. Therefore, to complain that God provides a way of forgiveness that glorifies his whole perfect nature is to impose our incomplete and often warped sense of glory upon the one true God.

On the other hand, a proper view of the atonement does not pit God's justice against his mercy. According to Scripture, God's provision of his own Son to bear our punishment and satisfy his own justice is simply the way in which God reveals his mercy and grace to us, without any disharmony in the perfection of the glory of his manifold attributes. When a sinner contemplates the cross of Christ, he therefore ought not complain that God has granted forgiveness through the satisfaction of his justice but instead must marvel that God should send his own Son to bear our just condemnation and in that way to grant us the unspeakable mercy of forgiveness through the blood of Christ.

Assessing the Criticism

In conclusion, I have identified four central criticisms of penal substitution, which, while not exhaustive of the literature, must surely be seen as representing the core complaints of non-violent atonement theologians against the traditional evangelical view. Classic evangelicals assert that while the cross may be well considered from an array of biblical perspectives, the chief and controlling biblical approach is penal substitution: Jesus Christ offered himself as a willing sacrifice, to suffer the penalty justly deserved by the sins of his people, dying on the cross in their place and receiving for them the wrath of the holy God. In so doing he displayed to the world God's matchless mercy and love so as to call for faith in Christ, grateful devotion to God, and the ethics of self-sacrificing love towards the world.

The critics assail this doctrine, complaining against the idea of divine wrath and retributive justice, asserting an objection based on inner-Trinitarian love, and maligning penal substitution as a perverse offense to the ethics taught by Jesus himself. If these criticisms can be biblically sustained, then penal substitution must indeed be set aside. But if these criticisms are unable to sustain the agreement of Holy Scripture—as they cannot—then God's Word calls for acceptance of penal substitution and the repentance of those who speak against this biblical teaching.

So vital is this issue to the whole range of Christian faith and experience that a sober and urgent call must go forth to embrace and espouse the Bible's own teaching of the cross of Christ, at the center of which is penal substitutionary atonement. And so central is this matter to the witness of Christianity in our times that biblically faithful evangelicals must agree with the conclusion offered by Garry Williams:

> I am mindful both of the injunctions of the Lord Jesus Christ to seek peace, and of the ways in which he and his apostles make clear that there are issues over which division is necessary. Does not the present debate over penal substitutionary atonement fall into this category of issues that require separation? I find it impossible to agree with those who maintain that the debate is just an intramural one which can be conducted within the evangelical family. . . . I cannot see how those who disagree can remain allied without placing unity about truths which are undeniably central to the Christian faith.[39]

Lastly, how can conventional evangelical Christians seek to understand the bases for the non-violent objection to penal substitution, involving an assault on what we consider to be the very heart of Christian faith and coupled with so many remarks that seem brazenly blasphemous and which previously have been heard only from lips that openly despise the cross? Are there observations that can be made with charitable honesty as to the sources of this non-violent theology of the atonement?

For starters, we might suspect an outworking of the low view of sin so prevalent in our culture. Surely this must play a role, since it is difficult to understand how anyone who feels the burden of his or her guilt before God's holiness could complain about the means by which God has shown us grace. Surely it follows that if God is not angry with our sin, then sin is not as abhorrent as we have been taught that it is. Furthermore, might this non-violent assault also reflect the results of an evangelical scholarship that has increasingly come under the spell of higher critical methods of Bible interpretation? In considering the recent treatment of biblical texts, such as Romans 1–3 and Isaiah 53, a traditional evangelical must indeed express dismay over the novel interpretations arising from complex hermeneutical maneuvers that result in the very objections long leveled against Christianity by liberal scholarship.

But I believe that the most telling explanation is seen in one of the criticisms that gains traction among many who are troubled by penal substitution. This complaint is that the classic evangelical doctrine of penal substitution results from Western standards of justice that have been thrust upon Christian thinking since medieval times. Just as medieval overlords imposed their rights with the edge of the sword, critics argue that this morality has not only been incorporated into subsequent Western judicial practice but also thrust upon the Scriptures. The problem, say critics like Joel Green and Mark Baker, is that traditional evangelicals have been unwittingly co-opted into worldly thinking about the cross; for instance, they express suspicion that penal substitution "coheres so fully with the emphasis on autonomous individualism characteristic of so much of the modern middle class in the West."[40]

Feeling the Weight of Sin

The correct reply to this line of concern is to point out that the model of judicial practice displayed in penal substitution is the farthest thing from what is practiced in courtrooms either in the West or anywhere else in the world. No Western court would ever direct that the guilt of a criminal be imputed to an innocent substitute, much less to the son of the judge, so that the substitute should receive punishment in the miscreant's place! Instead, if we reflect on the charge that penal substitution sets forth a moral atrocity—the charge leveled by its critics—we find that the very basis for their offense is the standards of judicial practice incorporated from the world. At its very core, the outrage against penal substitution is offense against the saving economy of God revealed in the Bible, on the basis of the morality and justice approved by the world.

In response to Green and Baker's concern that penal substitution smacks of Western individualism, Garry Williams is certainly on target when he replies: "This is a very strange line of criticism of penal substitution, since penal substitution itself relies on a denial of individualism."[41] He means that the underlying principle of penal substitution is the covenantal headship and representation of the Lord Jesus Christ. Penal substitution assumes not ultimate individualism but covenant solidarity through God's grace in Christ. Williams thus concludes: "There is an irony here. It is in fact the critics of penal substitution who have embraced individualism, not its proponents."[42]

He cites as an example the Church of England's 1995 Doctrine Commission report, The Mystery of Salvation, which insists that "in the moral sphere each person must be responsible for their own obligations. Moral responsibility is ultimately incommunicable." It is for this reason—an iron grip on Western individualism and its standards of justice—that the Church of England report rejects penal substitution.[43]

Any thorough study of the non-violent approach to Christ's atoning work, rejecting penal substitutionary atonement, will discover that it contains throughout a downplaying of sin, sin's dreadful consequences in God's judgment, and the infinite nature of sin's offense to our perfectly holy God. Therefore it will be only those people who feel the weight of their iniquity and guilt before God—sinners who can understand David's heart when he speaks of his bones wasting away through day-long groaning, and God's hand heavy upon him at night (Ps. 32:3–4)—who can not only embrace penal substitutionary atonement but rejoice in this truth of Christ's cross as our only hope. According to the faith of our evangelical fathers, such people, and they only, are properly called Christians.

But what about the culture? Is it true that our postmodern world does not register with the legal considerations of penal substitutionary atonement? If this is so, might it be that the world so little knows the truth about God and that our culture has, in its sensual addictions, as Paul puts it, suppressed the truth of God in unrighteousness and "exchanged the truth about God for a lie" (Rom. 1:18, 25)? If this is the case, and an assessment of postmodern culture based on a belief in the authority and truth of Scripture is bound to reach such a conclusion, then for Christians to collaborate in so deadly a deception will neither advance the true cause of the gospel nor reflect the merciful love of God towards the world.

But is it really true that the biblical gospel of Christ's atoning death as our penal substitute cannot hope to reach today's world? Once we see that the gospel reveals not another warmed-over version of failed humanistic thinking but, rather, a rejection of Western individualism for a saving, covenantal solidarity with God's own Son, who loved us enough even to take our sins to the cross, then perhaps Williams is right when he suggests that, contrary to its critics, "penal substitution has a bright future and will preach well."[44]

NOTES

Chapter 1: Necessary Blood

1. Scripture passages quoted in this chapter are taken from the King James Version of the Bible.
2. Horatius Bonar, "I Lay My Sins on Jesus" (1843).
3. Christina G. Rossetti, "None Other Lamb, None Other Name."
4. Unknown, "None but Christ."
5. Matthew Henry, *Commentary on the Whole Bible*, 6 vols. (Peabody, MA: Hendrickson, n.d.).

Chapter 3: Atoning Blood

1. *The Archbishop of Canterbury: William Tyndale; Reformer and Rebel. A Quincentenary Appreciation* (Lambeth Palace, October 5, 1994).
2. *Webster's Ninth New Collegiate Dictionary* (New York: Merriam-Webster, 1984), 113.
3. G. C. Berkouwer, *Faith and Justification* (Grand Rapids, MI: Eerdmans, 1954), 90.
4. Brad Jersak and Michael Hardin, eds., *Stricken by God? Nonviolent Identification and the Victory of Christ* (Grand Rapids, MI: Eerdmans, 2007), 14.
5. Jersak, in *Stricken by God?* 31.
6. Hardin, in *Stricken by God?* 55.
7. George Smeaton, *Christ's Doctrine of the Atonement* (Edinburgh, 1870; repr., Edinburgh: Banner of Truth, 1991), 1.
8. John Brown, *An Exposition of the Epistle of Paul the Apostle to the Galatians* (Edinburgh, 1853; repr., Evansville, IN: Sovereign Grace Book Club, 1957), 370.
9. Donald Macleod, *Faith to Live By* (Fearn, Ross-shire: Mentor, 1998), 129.
10. Tim Keller shared these questions with students at Westminster Theological Seminary (Philadelphia) in the syllabus for his course "Orientation to Ministry."
11. Anselm, in Gillian R. Evans, *Anselm*, Outstanding Christian Thinkers (Wilton, CT: Morehouse-Barlow, 1989), 29.
12. "There Is a Green Hill Far Away" (1848).
13. Thomas Cranmer, in *Right with God: Justification in the Bible and the World*, ed. D. A. Carson (London: World Evangelical Fellowship, 1992), 17.

14. John R. W. Stott, *The Cross of Christ* (Downers Grove, IL: InterVarsity, 1986), 190.
15. Cowper's story is recounted in F. W. Boreham, *A Bunch of Everlastings: Or Texts That Made History* (Philadelphia: Judson Press, 1920), 120–28.
16. Stott, 173.
17. Jersak, in *Stricken by God?* 27.
18. John Newton, entry for September 18, 1779, quoted in D. Bruce Hindmarsh, *John Newton and the English Evangelical Tradition* (Oxford: Oxford University Press, 1996), 232.
19. Stott, 175.
20. Wendy Murray Zoba, *Maya Mysteries*, quoted in *Books & Culture*, vol. 8, no. 1 (January/February 2002): 28.
21. Bill Maher, as interviewed on NBC's *Late Night with Conan O'Brien*.
22. William Still, *Dying to Live* (Fearn, Ross-shire: Christian Focus, 1991), 136.

Chapter 4: Cleansing Blood

1. Cf. R. Kent Hughes, *Ephesians: The Mystery of the Body of Christ* (Wheaton, IL: Crossway, 1990), 33.
2. From Psalm 51:1–15, "God, Be Merciful to Me," *The Psalter* (1912).
3. Augustus M. Toplady, "Rock of Ages, Cleft for Me" (1776).
4. William Cowper, "There Is a Fountain Filled with Blood" (1771).
5. John R. W. Stott, *The Cross of Christ* (Downers Grove, IL: InterVarsity, 1986), 167–203.
6. Ibid., 134.
7. Leon Morris, *The Apostolic Preaching of the Cross* (Grand Rapids, MI: Eerdmans, 1955, repr., 1992).
8. Along with Stott and Morris, this trend is seen in George Eldon Ladd, *A Theology of the New Testament* (Grand Rapids, MI: Eerdmans, 1974, rev. 1993), 470–74. A striking instance of this polemic against expiation is seen in Morris's treatment in J. D. Douglas, et al., *New Bible Dictionary* (Downers Grove, IL: InterVarsity, 1962), 362, in which Morris has nothing positive to say about expiation. More recently, balance has been restored with many evangelical writers acknowledging that atonement involves both propitiation and expiation.
9. Nancy Ganz, *Leviticus: A Commentary for Children*, Herein Is Love Commentary Series (Wapwollopen, PA: Shepherd Press, 2002), 30.
10. Ibid.
11. Charles H. Spurgeon, *The Metropolitan Tabernacle Pulpit: Sermons Preached and Revised by C. H. Spurgeon*, 31:438–39.
12. Cited from Don Stephens, *War and Grace* (Darlington, UK: Evangelical Press, 2005), 253–71.

Chapter 7: Early Church Reflections

1. The exact division of this period can vary. Thus, in a recent five-volume edition covering church history from Christ to the present day, the division is made

at Emperor Constantine rather than, say, at the death of Augustine in AD 430 or the beginning of the medieval era in AD 600. Cf. Ivor J. Davidson, *The Birth of the Church: From Jesus to Constantine, AD 30–312*, The Baker History of the Church, vol. 1, ed. Tim Dowley (Grand Rapids, MI: Baker, 2004); *A Public Faith: From Constantine to the Medieval World*, The Baker History of the Church, vol. 2, ed. Tim Dowley (Grand Rapids, MI: Baker, 2005).

2. B. B. Warfield, "Augustine," in *Calvin and Augustine*, ed. Samuel G. Craig (Philadelphia: P&R, 1980), 322. "For the Reformation, inwardly considered, was just the triumph of Augustine's doctrine of grace over Augustine's doctrine of the Church."

3. Cf. Robert Letham, *Through Western Eyes: Eastern Orthodoxy: A Reformed Perspective* (Fearn, Ross-shire: Mentor, 2007), 243–70.

4. On the nature of theology (dogma) as a "science," see James Orr, *The Progress of Dogma* (Grand Rapids, MI: Eerdmans, 1960 [1952]), 1–32; Jaroslav Pelikan, *The Christian Tradition: A History of the Development of Doctrine*, 5 vols. (Chicago: The University of Chicago Press, 1971–1989); Geoffrey Bromiley, *Historical Theology: An Introduction* (Grand Rapids, MI: Eerdmans, 1978); L. Berkhof, *The History of Christian Doctrines* (London: Banner of Truth, 1969 [1939]).

5. The lack of debate on the atonement in the early church can be evidenced, for example, by examining the chapters of a recent book in which theological issues in the early church are in view: there are chapters on the person of Christ, the Trinity, the Holy Spirit, grace and the human condition, God's transcendence, and the doctrine of providence, but nothing on the death of Christ or the atonement. See, Christopher Hill, *Learning Theology with the Church Fathers* (Downers Grove, IL: InterVarsity, 2002).

6. See J. B. Lightfoot, ed., *The Apostolic Fathers* (Grand Rapids, MI: Baker, 1965).

7. Henry Chadwick, *The Early Church* (London: Penguin, 1974), 38–40.

8. See Eric Osborn, *Irenaeus of Lyons* (Cambridge: Cambridge University Press, 2001), 97–116; Robert Grant, *Irenaeus of Lyons* (London; New York: Routledge, 1997), 46–56.

9. See Irenaeus's *Adversus Haereses*, book 2, In *Against Heresies*, trans. A Roberts and W. H. Rambaut, ANCL, 5.9 (1883–84).

10. See Robert Letham, *The Work of Christ* (Leicester: Inter-Varsity, 1993), chap. 8.

11. Gustav Aulén, *Christus Victor* (London: SPCK, 1931). For an example of just how popular this view has become since the work of Gustav Aulén a century ago, see Hans Boersma, *Violence, Hospitality and the Cross* (Grand Rapids, MI: Baker Books, 2004). The book is not without its problems, but Boersma's thesis in part is to argue that violence is an unavoidable aspect of redemption in a fallen world.

12. See "Atonement," in John Anthony McGuckin, *The Westminster Handbook to Patristic Theology* (Louisville, London: Westminster John Knox, 2004), 36–39.

230

13. See Donald Macleod, *The Person of Christ* (Leicester: Inter-Varsity, 1998), 121–54.
14. "Homily XI" (2 Corinthians 5:11), *Nicene and Post-Nicene Fathers*, Series 1, ed. Philip Schaff (Peabody, MA: Hendrickson, 1994).

Chapter 8: The Medieval Achievement

1. Gillian R. Evans, *Anselm*, Outstanding Christian Thinkers (Wilton, CT: Morehouse–Barlow, 1989), 2.
2. Ibid., 5.
3. R. W. Southern, *Anselm: A Portrait in a Landscape* (Cambridge: Cambridge UP, 1990), 70.
4. Evans, *vii.*
5. *Proslogion* as quoted in Stephen J. Nichols, *Pages from Church History: A Guided Tour of Christian Classics* (Phillipsburg, NJ: P&R, 2006), 87.
6. Ibid., 98.
7. Evans, 9, paraphrasing Anselm's *Letter 112.*
8. Nichols, 99.
9. Evans, *ix.*
10. Ibid.
11. Ibid., *x.*
12. Ibid., 50.
13. Ibid., 51.
14. *Proslogion*, in Nichols, 106.
15. Evans, 29.
16. Ibid., 25.
17. Anselm, *Cur Deus Homo* (Edinburgh: John Grant, 1909), 4.
18. Ibid., 5.
19. Nichols, 101.
20. Anselm, *Cur Deus Homo*, 12–14.
21. Ibid., 50.
22. Ibid., 49.
23. Ibid., 45.
24. Ibid., 55.
25. Nichols, 103–4.
26. Nichols, 104.
27. Anselm, *Cur Deus Homo?* 99–100.
28. Jaroslav Pelikan, *The Christian Tradition: A History of the Development of Doctrine*, vol. 4, *Reformation of Church and Dogma (1300–1700)* (Chicago: University of Chicago Press, 1984), 156–57.
29. All quotes from Pelikan, 23–25.
30. Robert B. Strimple, "St. Anselm's *Cur deus homo* and John Calvin's *Doctrine of the Atonement*," in D. E. Luscombe and G. R. Evans, *Anselm: Aosta, Bec and Canterbury* (Sheffield: Sheffield Academic Press, 1996), 354.

31. John Calvin, *Institutes of the Christian Religion*, ed. John T. McNeill, trans. Ford Lewis Battles, 2 vols., Library of Christian Classics (Philadelphia: Westminster, 1960), 2.12.3.
32. Ibid., 2.15.6.
33. Strimple, 354–57.
34. Ibid., 357–59.
35. William Neil, *Apostle Extraordinary* (London: Religious Education Press, 1965), 89–90.
36. Brad Jersak and Michael Hardin, *Stricken by God? Nonviolent Identification and the Victory of Christ* (Grand Rapids, MI: Eerdmans, 2007), endorsement.
37. Ibid., 253.
38. Ibid., 29–30.
39. Anselm, "A Meditation of Human Redemption," in *Anselm of Canterbury*, ed. and trans. J. Hopkins and H. Richardson (New York: Dorling Kindersley, 1974), 139–40.
40. Anselm, *Cur Deus Homo?* 58.
41. Ibid., 106.

Chapter 9: The Reformation Consensus

1. John Calvin, *Sermons on the Epistle to the Ephesians* (Edinburgh: Banner of Truth, 1562; repr., 1973), 51.
2. Ibid.
3. Ibid., 51–52.
4. Ibid., 55.
5. Nikolaus Ludwig von Zinzendorf, "Jesus, Thy Blood and Righteousness" (1739).

Chapter 10: The Blood of Christ in Puritan Piety

1. Stephen Charnock, *The Works of Stephen Charnock*, vol. 4, *The Knowledge of God* (Edinburgh: Banner of Truth, 1985), 506.
2. Stephen Charnock, "The Cleansing Virtue of Christ's Blood," in *The Works of Stephen Charnock*, vol. 3, *The New Birth* (Edinburgh: Banner of Truth, 1986), 501–34, and "The Knowledge of Christ Crucified," *Works of Charnock*, 4:494–506; Thomas Goodwin, "Reconciliation by the Blood of Christ," *The Works of Thomas Goodwin* (Grand Rapids, MI: Reformation Heritage, 2006), 5:499–521; Isaac Ambrose, *Looking Unto Jesus* (Harrisonburg, VA: Sprinkle Publications, 1986). Cf. David Clarkson, "Christ's Dying for Sinners," in *The Works of David Clarkson* (Edinburgh: Banner of Truth, 1988), 3:63–80; Thomas Manton, "The Blood of Sprinkling," in *The Complete Works of Thomas Manton* (London: J. Nisbet, 1875), 22:106–22; Samuel Rutherford, *Christ Dying and Drawing Sinners to Himself* (London: Andrew Crooks, 1647); James Durham, "Remission of Sins Is Through Christ's Blood Alone," in *The Unsearchable Riches of Christ* (Morgan, PA: Soli Deo Gloria, 2002), 306–40; John Owen, "The Doctrine of Justification by Faith, through the Imputation of

the Righteousness of Christ," in *The Works of John Owen,* vol. 5 (Edinburgh: Banner of Truth, 1999).

3. For a helpful study on the biblical usage of the word *blood,* see Leon Morris, *The Apostolic Preaching of the Cross* (Grand Rapids, MI: Eerdmans, 1965), 112–28.

4. See Joel R. Beeke, "Calvin's Piety," in *The Cambridge Companion to John Calvin,* ed. Donald K. McKim (Cambridge: Cambridge University Press, 2004), 125–52.

5. Goodwin, *Works of Thomas Goodwin,* 5:501.

6. Charnock, *Works of Stephen Charnock,* 3:518.

7. Ibid., 3:505.

8. Ibid., 3:519.

9. Ibid.

10. Ibid., 3:521.

11. Ibid., 3:522.

12. Ibid., 3:505–6.

13. Ibid., 3:519.

14. *Works of Thomas Goodwin,* 5:509.

15. Ambrose, *Looking Unto Jesus,* 381–82.

16. Ibid., 385.

17. Charnock, *Works of Stephen Charnock,* 3:521.

18. Ibid., 3:518.

19. Ibid., 3:522.

20. Ibid., 3:518.

21. Ibid., 3:504.

22. Ibid., 4:504–5.

23. Ibid., 4:505.

24. Ibid.

25. Ibid., 4:505–6.

26. Ibid., 4:506.

27. Ibid., 3:516.

28. Ibid., 3:515–16.

29. Ibid., 3:516.

30. Ibid., 4:503.

31. Ambrose, *Looking Unto Jesus,* 384.

32. Charnock, *Works of Stephen Charnock,* 3:522–23.

33. Ibid., 3:523.

34. Ambrose, *Looking Unto Jesus,* 382.

35. Ibid., 372.

36. Goodwin, *Works of Thomas Goodwin,* 5:516.

37. Charnock, *Works of Stephen Charnock,* 3:531–34.

Chapter 12: Penal Substitutionary Atonement

1. John Shelby Spong, *Why Christianity Must Change or Die* (San Francisco: HarperCollins, 1999), 95.

2. Steve Chalke, *The Lost Message of Jesus* (Grand Rapids, MI: Zondervan, 2003), 182.

3. Joel B. Green and Mark D. Baker, *Recovering the Scandal of the Cross: Atonement in New Testament and Contemporary Contexts* (Downers Grove, IL: InterVarsity, 2000), 30.

4. Brad Jersak and Michael Hardin, *Stricken by God? Nonviolent Identification and the Victory of Christ* (Grand Rapids, MI: Eerdmans, 2007), 55.

5. Ibid., 65.

6. J. I. Packer, "What Did the Cross Achieve? The Logic of Penal Substitution," in J. I. Packer and Mark Dever, *In My Place Condemned He Stood: Celebrating the Glory of the Atonement* (Wheaton, IL: Crossway, 2007), 53.

7. See pp. 47–48 in this volume.

8. Green and Baker, *Recovering the Scandal of the Cross*, 23.

9. Ibid., 220–21.

10. Cited in J. Denny Weaver, *The Nonviolent Atonement* (Grand Rapids, MI: Eerdmans, 2001), 129.

11. Jersak and Hardin, *Stricken by God?* 19.

12. Green and Baker, *Recovering the Scandal of the Cross*, 51.

13. Ibid., 150.

14. Jersak and Hardin, *Stricken by God?* 23.

15. Gregory A. Boyd, in James Beilby and Paul R. Eddy, *The Nature of the Atonement* (Downers Grove, IL: InterVarsity, 2006), 104.

16. Joel B. Green, in Beilby and Eddy, *The Nature of the Atonement,* 114; emphasis added.

17. Sharon Baker, in Jersak and Hardin, *Stricken by God?* 222–23.

18. Steve Chalke, *Lost Message*, 182–83.

19. Jersak and Hardin, *Stricken by God?* 73.

20. J. Denny Weaver, *The Nonviolent Atonement* (Grand Rapids, MI: Eerdmans, 2001), 225.

21. Ibid., 225.

22. I. Howard Marshall, "The Theology of the Atonement," in *The Atonement Debate: Papers from the London Symposium on the Theology of the Atonement,* ed. Derek Tidball, David Hilborn, and Justin Thacker (Grand Rapids, MI: Zondervan, 2008), 51.

23. Green and Baker, *Recovering the Scandal of the Cross*, 54–55.

24. Cited in J. I. Packer, "The Heart of the Gospel," in Packer and Dever, *In My Place Condemned*, 35.

25. John R. W. Stott, *The Cross of Christ* (Downers Grove, IL: InterVarsity, 1986), 106.

26. Ibid., 106.

27. Ibid., 173.

28. Tidball, et al., *The Atonement Debate*, 53–54.

29. Packer and Dever, *In My Place Condemned*, 35.

30. Stephen H. Travis, *Christ and the Judgment of God: Divine Retribution in the New Testament* (Basingstoke: Marshall Pickering, 1986), Preface.

31. Garry J. Williams, "Penal Substitution: A Response to Recent Criticisms," in Tidball, et al., *The Atonement Debate*, 175.
32. Ibid., 176–77.
33. Ibid., 177.
34. Ibid., 178.
35. Steve Chalke, *Lost Message*, 182–83.
36. Packer and Dever, *In My Place Condemned*, 89.
37. Tidball, et al., *The Atonement Debate*, 178.
38. Ibid., 62.
39. Ibid., 188.
40. Green and Baker, *Recovering the Scandal*, 213.
41. Tidball, et al., *The Atonement Debate*, 181.
42. Ibid., 182.
43. Church of England, *The Mystery of Salvation* (London: Church House, 1995), 212.
44. Tidball, et al., *The Atonement Debate*, 183.

GENERAL INDEX

Abelard, Peter, 120, 138
Alexander, Cecil Frances, 54
Ambrose, Isaac, 169, 170, 175, 177, 178, 231n, 232n
Amyraldianism, 165–66, 186–89
Amyraut, Moses, 186, 207
Anselm of Canterbury, 52, 120, 147; vs. Abelard, 138; archbishop, 126; attacks on, 140–41; *Cur Deus Homo*, 127, 129–37; death of, 129; Eadmer's biography, 123; greatness of, 123; humility of, 124; influence of, 139; life of, 124; ontological proof, 127–28; piety of, 125; on prayer, 128–29; Proslogion, 127; teaching on sin, 133–35; writings of, 127
Aquinas, Thomas, 147
Arminianism, and the atonement, 184; origin of, 184
Arminius, Jacob, 184–85
Armstrong, Brian, 186
Athenasius, 117, 120
atonement, active obedience of Christ, 91–92, 140, 169, 170, 185; Amyraldian challenge, 186–89; for any sin, 44, 177; at-one-ment, 48; attacks against, 49, 67, 182–203, 206–25; basis of forgiveness, 80, 168; blood of Christ, 23, 58, 61–62, 71, 155, 164; Calvin on, 139; centrality of, 49, 112; Christus Victory theory, 116, 118–20, 131, 208; cleansed conscience, 75–80; confessional creeds, 111; "cosmic child abuse," 206; Day of, 57; debt paid, 133–34; divine decrees, 187–89; early church views, 112–21; efficacy of, 197–99, 201; expiation (cleansing from sin), 66–80, 166–67; extent of, 159–61; glory of, 131, 155; governmental theory of, 194–96; humbling effects of, 176; "limited," 159–61, 197–98; Mayan practice of, 61–62; mercy seat, 58–60, 176; morality of, 192; moral example theory, 138; necessity of, 16–19,

23, 34, 50, 62, 132–34, 175, 202; "nonviolent" atonement, 209–11, 223–25; offense of, 205; Old Testament fulfilled, 16, 67; once for all, 148–49, 181, 183; passive obedience of Christ, 170, 185; pastoral implications of, 182; pastoral implications of, 203; pedagogy of, 114; penal substitution, 120–21, 134, 140, 192–93, 207–9, 217–25; personal and individual, 23; precious blood, 97–106, 138; and propitiation (wrath averted), 23, 31, 34, 56–60, 69, 71, 138, 140; ransom, 115–16, 118–22, 131–32, 169; recapitulation theory, 114, 117; received by faith, 44, 170–71, 201; reconciliation, God's way of, 60; relationship to incarnation, 137; retributive justice, 209–10, 220; sacrificial death, 100; sanctifying effects of, 172–73; satisfaction of justice, 134–37, 169, 173; satisfaction for sin, 50–52, 135–37, 139, 142, 169, 172–73; imputation of, 58, 167–68, 201; and social violence, 210; substitutionary, 19–20, 24, 42, 60, 167; suffering servant, 102; thanksgiving for, 62–63; *theopoiesis*, 116; therapeutic model of, 208; trusting in, 78; Tyndale's invention, 47–48; vicarious sacrifice, 20, 58; voluntary sacrifice, 132, 138; unpopular doctrine, 48, 84–91
Augustine, bishop of Hippo, 94, 110, 116, 124, 132
Aulen, Gustav, 116, 229n
Baker, Mark D., 206, 208–9, 223–24, 233n, 234n
Baker, Sharon, 210, 233n
Battles, Ford Lewis, 231n
Baxter, Richard, 196, 199–202
Beeke, Joel, 232n
Bellarmine, Robert, 165
Berkof, Louis, 110, 229n
Berkouwer, G. C., 48, 227n
Beza, Theodore, 184

SCRIPTURE INDEX